understanding Teenagers

A GUIDE FOR PARENTS

James J. DiGiacomo, S.J.
Edward Wakin

Argus Communications
A Division of DLM, Inc.
Allen, Texas 75002 U.S.A.

ACKNOWLEDGMENTS

Score-It-Yourself Quiz from *Young People and A.A.* reprinted with permission of Alcoholics Anonymous World Services, Inc.

Excerpt from *How to Make Your Child a Winner* by Victor B. Cline. Copyright © 1980 by the author. Used by permission of Walker & Co.

Excerpt from lyrics for "Angry Young Man" by Billy Joel. © 1976 & 1979 Blackwood Music Inc. Used by permission. All rights reserved.

Excerpt from *When It's Time to Talk about Sex* by Gordon J. Lester. Copyright © 1981, St. Meinrad Archabbey, St. Meinrad, IN 47477. Copies may be ordered through the publisher, Abbey Press, St. Meinrad, IN 47577.

Excerpts from *The New York Times.* © 1978/81 by The New York Times Company. Reprinted by permission.

Excerpts from *The Private Life of the American Teenager* by Jane Norman and Myron W. Harris. Copyright © 1981 Jane Norman and Myron Harris, Ph.D. Reprinted with the permission of Rawson, Wade Publishers, Inc.

Excerpts from *A New Generation* by Michael Novak. Copyright © 1964 by Michael Novak. Reprinted with adaptation by permission of the author.

Excerpt from *Values and Teaching* by Louis Raths, Merrill Harmin, and Sidney Simon. Reprinted by permission of the publisher, Charles F Merrill Publishing Co.

Excerpt from "Why Parents Can't Say Enough About Sex," *U.S. Catholic,* October 1982. Reprinted by permission.

Excerpts from *Youth and the Future of the Church* by Michael Warren. Copyright © 1982 by The Seabury Press. Used by permission.

PHOTO CREDITS

Paul Conklin   76
Evan Johnson/JEROBOAM   4
Ed Lettau/PHOTO RESEARCHERS, INC.   130
Monique Manceau/PHOTO RESEARCHERS, INC.   58
Mike Norcia/SYGMA   22
Jim Richardson/BLACK STAR   114
Rose Skytta/JEROBOAM   98
W. D. Zehr/FPG   36

Designed by Tricia Legault

Printed in the United States of America

Argus Communications
A Division of DLM, Inc.
One DLM Park
Allen, Texas 75002 U.S.A.

International Standard Book Number: 0-89505-129-X
Library of Congress Catalog Card Number: 83-70289
0 9 8 7 6 5 4 3 2 1

CONTENTS

Introduction

Ten years ago, in another book, we looked at the stormy relations between parents and children—the "generation gap"—and explored the questions and issues involving young Americans. Parents and educators were asking with varying degrees of confusion, rage, curiosity, and goodwill, "What do these kids want?"

Teenagers answered: "We don't want what you want."

Adults: "That's no answer."

Teenagers: "We want to be left alone. We want to be free."

Adults: "Freedom *from* is not enough. You must be free *for* something."

Then came slogans and criticism, rebukes and rhetoric, warfare at the dinner table and loud music in the bedroom. It became a frustrating dialogue of the deaf.

Drawing on our experiences with both teenagers and parents, we tried to get in the middle by discussing what was at stake, what was at issue, and what could be done.

We called our book *We Were Never Their Age* to underline (1) the reality that each generation has its own unique experience in the life cycle and (2) the rapid rate of social change that was bringing young people into a radically different American setting. Old rules, familiar guidelines,

1

and standard maps seemed of little use. Church, home, and country were scorned by the very sons and daughters who benefited from the struggles of fathers and mothers determined that their children would have it "better." Parents in turn were disappointed and shocked when teenagers rejected the parental version of that better life.

Yesterday, when parents and teenagers were pitted against each other, they seemed to find it impossible to listen to each other. They argued. The words were angry, the behavior rebellious. The gap often seemed unbridgeable and there was a demand for bridge building. Thus our earlier book.

Today, parents are still asking about how to communicate with teenage sons and daughters. Educators, too, wonder about teenagers. Adults, in general, still wonder what teenagers want or whether they really want anything passionately. Teenagers once asked with idealistic fire, "Where have all the flowers gone?" Today, adults ask, "Where has all the enthusiasm gone?" Parents are readier to listen, but teenagers seem to be saying less than ever.

One qualification immediately: yesterday, the stereotypes of teenagers were overdone with considerable help from the mass media. There was plenty of overreaction amidst the popular images of teenagers. Today, the image of teenagers as apathetic, listless high school students is just as overdone. What anyone says about teenagers in general must be evaluated by each parent and teacher to determine what applies to specific teenagers.

One dynamic, however, applies to both yesterday and today and to all teenagers: the pulling away of teenagers and the reaching out of parents. In that sense, there is bound to be a generation gap, and this gap occurs in a dramatically different context from one generation to the next. The times have changed once again, and *we are still not their age.*

Today's differences prompted us to examine what is happening, starting with the realization of how much has changed. We reviewed what we have learned about the process of reaching out to teenagers in the past decade and examined the current context for dialogue and meaningful relations. The need to communicate is as great as ever, a conviction reinforced by contacts with teenagers and parents all around the country. A different context calls for a new book—this one.

We have been encouraged to write another book as a result of the questions, concerns, and often direct requests of parents. We find that our earlier book is still remembered by parents who have said in one way or another: "It's time for you to write another book about teenagers and parents."

Rereading the reviews of our earlier book also encouraged us. Like all authors, we relish the favorable comments: "Some parents and educators need this book more than others, but all can learn from it." "This easy-reading volume provides a deeply serious goad to both thought and conscience and should become as valuable a source book for the teacher and religious education teacher as for parents." "The authors raise all the questions parents worry about and answer them frankly from their wide experience with young people." ". . . both helpful and enriching." ". . . practical without being preachy, entertaining without being flip." "The parent comes away from it with the keys to the future" of his or her teenager.

So here it is, a totally new book drawing on a range of new material provided by social scientists, educators, researchers, and, of course, parents and teenagers. Add countless numbers of conversations and experiences accumulated over the past ten years.

Our goal, however, remains the same. We aim at the kind of success all of us in the older generation really want in our relations with the young—to prepare them to live not in our past but in their future.

ot Exactly the Time
of Their Lives

Scenes change dramatically from one teen generation to another.

In an earlier generation, a TV camera zoomed in on a long-haired teenager in T-shirt and jeans who flashed a V-for-victory sign and waved a picket sign that read "Stop _____" or "Free _____." Or a photographer captured the familiar scene of teenagers establishing instant community by passing a marijuana joint around. It was a teenage world of *Revolution for the Hell of It* as proclaimed by Yippie media star Abbie Hoffman.

In the current generation, the standard scene is likely to be a teenager hunched over Pac-Man or any of the other video games in the $5-billion-a-year industry. Or teenagers walking side by side, lost in private worlds of music provided by the headphones of their Walkmans.

In the early 1970s, the "system" was the enemy and its daily irritant was high school. Many of the best and the brightest students devoted themselves to fighting the status quo. By the early 1980s, teenagers were accepting the "system" (the word itself is passé) and were more likely to criticize themselves.

Two high school voices a decade apart illustrate the difference. The first is Michael Marqusee, writing as leader of

radical students in the stronghold of suburban affluence—
Scarsdale, New York. The year was 1970.

> No creativity, no individuality, no questioning.
> We seem to be merely manipulated by a system
> (not by other individuals), from point to point
> with no purpose. Many of us feel powerless. Our
> only avenue to true self-expression and devel-
> opment is through rebellion against the society
> that created that monstrosity: Plastic Man. By crit-
> icizing and ultimately destroying this form of life
> we hope to free man from all kinds of oppression:
> economic, racial, cultural. Thus, here I am, an
> affluent radical, the most bourgeois of contra-
> dictions.[1]

The second voice is Susan Freiwald, editorializing in the
Red & White, a highly regarded newspaper at the presti-
gious San Francisco Lowell High School. The year was
1982.

> High school is like a set of headphones.
> Although at times the music it plays is construc-
> tive or educational, it provides a shelter and,
> therefore, isolation. In the same way that a per-
> son with headphones on cannot talk with others,
> a high school student cuts himself off from new
> ideas and listens only to familiar sounds.

How did Susan come to think of headphones as a meta-
phor for high school? Her answer is revealing.

> One afternoon I was walking down the hall,
> and here all these kids were sitting in the hall
> next to each other, not talking to each other,
> shutting each other out, listening to music on
> their Walkmans.

---

[1]Michael Marqusee, "Turn Left at Scarsdale," in *The High School Revolutionaries,* Marc Libarle and Tom Seligson, eds. (New York: Random House, 1970), p. 23.

Early in the 1980s, one of the few protests visible in local communities was parental. The target was video games, and the outcome was local ordinances restricting young people from playing them in public. One Long Islander, Ronnie Lamm, gained national publicity with her campaign against them. Video arcades were denounced as centers for drug dealing, drinking, and gambling. Mrs. Lamm accused the games of encouraging "aggressive behavior" and complained that "hours of staring into the machine" decreased the ability to communicate.

The complaint was symbolic.

Teenagers are no longer viewed as dangerous activists, but as passive bystanders.

Teenagers are no longer looked upon as creating a turbulent world of their own, but as shutting themselves up in bland isolation.

Teenagers are no longer celebrated as "doing their own thing" and flying high, but as not knowing what they want to do and walking slowly.

Along with these changes in the image of teenagers, there has been a shift of attention: teenagers went out of season as far as the media and public attention were concerned. (*Time* magazine announced in 1981: "Compared with their predecessors, Americans in the pre-adult age brackets have, for the past ten years, been nearly invisible.") But not as far as millions of parents are concerned.

A Time of Turmoil

More than 32 million young people in the thirteen-to-twenty-one age group are living through the most intense, explosive part of the life cycle, whether or not the media are watching. Teenagers are in the period of life when everything is bigger than normal scale, when each physical, psychological, emotional, and mental breakthrough is bigger, brighter, more intense, more special than it will ever be again.

The teen years are a first time for so many things, and the first time in everything is always special. Moreover, since each new generation of teenagers is so much more precocious than the previous one, the list of firsts becomes longer for each succeeding generation. Hardly anything of personal consequence seems to wait until the teen years are over. This means that each succeeding generation of teenagers puts new pressures on parents.

The challenges facing teenagers and their parents divide into two:

1. Challenges arising from the explosive teenage experience itself. They will always be there.
2. Challenges arising from society, the mass media, and the social-economic facts of American life. They keep changing.

Together, the challenges shape the teenage time of life. No teenager (or parent) can escape either what comes from the passage into adulthood or what comes from the environment. Of course, not all the pressures of American society hit each teenager in the same way. But generalizations do serve a purpose by pointing out the patterns that seem to be visible among teenagers. It is up to each parent to weigh generalizations and determine how they apply to their teenagers. The same is true of teachers and anyone else in close contact with teenagers.

As the bridge between childhood and adulthood, teenage years represent a time of transition from being dependent to being independent. Because teenagers are no longer holding their parents' hand and are not yet standing on their own feet, there is a tug between holding on and breaking away. That unavoidable tension is bound to complicate relations between parents and teenagers.

Physically, teenagers may look like adults, but psychologically they are still feeling their way with regard to freedom and independence. Their feelings are fragile and their reactions are volatile as their bodies undergo the most rapid and dramatic growth in the entire life cycle (except for the first year of life). The movement into puberty ushers in a host of changes and a string of questions, doubts, and concerns about the body, about health, and in particular about *what is normal.*

8

Teenagers worry about being too short, too tall, too thin, too fat, about being underdeveloped or overdeveloped. Because each teenager develops on a different timetable, that worry afflicts all teenagers to some extent. Their bodies are exploding and changing dramatically at a time when they are acutely conscious about themselves as social beings. They can't help comparing themselves with other teenagers, and such comparisons can bedevil them.

At the same time, with each passing year teenagers face increasing pressure to prepare for adult life by doing well in high school and by making decisions and plans. One part of them wants to be *free;* the other part has trouble coping with the responsibilities that come with freedom.

So all at once, teenagers are —

- coming to terms with their own bodies,
- working out relationships with other teenagers,
- reaching for independence from their parents,
- laying the groundwork for adult life, particularly in planning careers,
- asserting their own individual way of looking at life.

The trip is bound to be bumpy. In fact, strain and stress are important in the growing-up process. Teenagers who don't confront their own limitations and who don't learn to deal with their problems prolong childhood rather than prepare for adulthood. Dr. Robert Coles of Harvard University, celebrated for his ability to tune in on young people and describe their inner lives, made this point in a discussion of the teen years.

> Part of growing up is realizing one's uniqueness, realizing one's finitude and experiencing disappointment and sadness. There is no way of avoiding them. Loneliness is what we all experience as human beings. Who would want to tell us that we are not going to experience loneliness? That is part of what it is to be a human being—to know one's limitations, to experience

disappointments, and also just to feel at times apart from others. At times, to be lonely is to be alive.[2]

Loneliness, self-doubt, frustration, and anxiety are painful and private experiences. Teenagers do not tell their parents about them in direct news reports that announce: "Gee, Mom, I'm feeling lonely, left out" or "Hey, Dad, know what? I'm feeling anxious about my future." Part of being a teenager is being private; another part is the need to sort out explosive physical and emotional changes. The teen years are experiential rather than analytical, a time of learning to ride the waves by diving in and thrashing around. Teenagers need to know that parents are standing by, ready and willing to help, but they don't want to face a district attorney at dinner.

Teenagers can change moods suddenly as they get caught up in the churning emotions of growing up. They can then baffle, confound, even anger parents who want to help but are kept away by surliness, sullenness, and tight-lipped silence. The reminder that "this too shall pass" is not particularly comforting as parents confront teenage emotional storms. But watchful waiting and patience still work best.

One young woman in her twenties looked back into her recent past to describe the confusion about her feelings. Often, she was not sure what was bothering her, where it came from, and why it was so upsetting. As she grew older, her feelings did not change. Rather, she became clearer about what they were. "The difference between then and now," she says, "is that *then* I didn't know what I was suffering from. It was hard to really be in touch with any of my emotions. I just felt them. If I was aware of my emotions, I was too proud to admit them to someone else. There is a great fear of being different at that age, yet becoming an individual is what each of us is supposed to be doing."

---

[2]Personal interview with one of the authors (Edward Wakin).

10

Major Influences on Teenage Life

What counts in the American teenage experience is other teenagers. By the time an adolescent reaches age fifteen, other teenagers dominate both family and school in influencing and absorbing his or her energies. School takes the most time and makes the most demands, but fellow teenagers command the most attention and rate as most important.

In short, the American teenage experience means that parents must cope with increasing independence on the part of their teenagers and decreasing control on their own part. That is the challenge built into the process of being a parent of any teenager.

When parents complain of a cold shoulder from sons and daughters, they ignore the teenage message: *I need to find my own space.* Actually, much more communication takes place than either parent or teenager acknowledges. Heart-to-heart talks are reassuring for parents, but meaningful communication takes place with looks, sighs, grunts, or is slipped in (during a discussion of a ball game, a new car, an event on the block). Actually, communications in the family never cease as parents and children fill the home with silent language about how they feel, react, think, hope, and fear. Parents and children know much more about each other than they realize. Only in the long run does the encyclopedia of mutual knowledge become apparent.

Teenagers even admit—to strangers—that they can communicate with their parents. For example, an extensive survey of 160,000 teenagers reported that—

- 83 percent of the teenagers said they can at least sometimes tell one or both parents how they think and feel.
- 60 percent said parents listen and care about their ideas and opinions, though 40 percent thought their parents do not care.[3]

---

[3]Jane Norman and Myron W. Harris, *The Private Life of the American Teenager* (New York: Rawson, Wade Publishers, 1981), p. 5.

While social scientists and commentators talk in terms of surveys and spout generalizations about teenagers as a whole, parents think of specific teenagers—their own. Generalizations are useful when they clarify teenage attitudes and behavior and help parents understand what is going on. At the same time that each teenager is different and distinctive, all teenagers breathe the same air in America's media-saturated culture. No one is immune to the environment.

Teenagers are particularly susceptible to cues from the mass media. They are omnivorous consumers of everything from horror movies to "Top 100" records, from commercials to TV adventure series. Since they are wired to each other by the vast apparatus of media, it is hardly surprising that teenagers all over the country resemble each other. The dynamic is basic: *same stage of life, same influences, similar reactions.*

The pressures of the media and of peers close in on teenagers. The media are telling them what is "in" and what other teenagers are doing, buying, saying, eating, trying. Teenagers do not want to be left out; they want to be "in." They are getting the same instructions, all the more effective because the instructions are not like orders from those in official authority. The report that "everyone is doing it" is much more commanding than a direct order.

Ironically, during the countercultural sixties, when teenagers were bent on doing their "own thing," they were conformists in the way they rebelled—the same clothes, the same long hair, the same folk heroes, the same V sign, the same joint. Those who held the mike, seized the spotlight, and captured the headlines did the cueing. Their anchorman was not Walter Cronkite but Bob Dylan.

Both Vulnerable and Susceptible

The underlying lesson of the sixties and the eighties is that American teenagers are both vulnerable and susceptible. The dangers in the larger society weigh in upon them, reminding them how vulnerable they are. Their response to social fashions show how susceptible they are.

In the sixties, the Vietnam war and the draft showed young Americans how vulnerable they are. Their media-sponsored heroes demonstrated how susceptible they are to social fashions. The reaction was rebellious.

In the eighties, the threat of nuclear war, as well as the tightening of economic opportunities, is sending the vulnerability message. Teenagers are showing their susceptibility by turning vocational and prudent. The reaction is conformist.

The flip-flop is personified by Jerry Rubin, one of the most defiant rebels of the sixties. He ended that decade by publishing another in the string of outrageous books by the hippie-yippie folk heroes. He wrote *We Are Everywhere* while serving sixty days in Chicago's Cook County Jail after being charged with inciting to riot and contempt of court. In the book, he cited letters from "beautiful young people" that "reveal the breakdown of America." He added: "The money the publishers will pay me for this book will be used to destroy Cook County Jail and every other jail and penitentiary in America." He was exultant, defiant, and determined to "destroy capitalist, Christian culture."[4]

By the 1980s, Rubin had reemerged as a stockbroker and had established a "Business Networking Salon" as "a high-level way for successful men and women to meet one another, make important connections, and expand their business and personal opportunities in the 1980s." He hailed Business Networking as "an excellent opportunity for financiers, artists, entrepreneurs, corporate executives, producers, clients, writers and deal-makers to meet one another in a fun and relaxed environment." One other thing, he noted: "As American Express is now accepted at Studio 54, you may charge this business-social experience to your company."[5]

With former revolutionary leaders like that, no wonder conformism seems rampant in the eighties. From Rubin

---

[4]Jerry Rubin, *We Are Everywhere* (New York: Harper & Row, 1971), pp. 8, 254.
[5]Flier mailed out by Jerry Rubin.

the revolutionary to Rubin the "business networker," from picketing to Pac-Man, from dropping out to putting on headphones, the setting for teenage life has changed dramatically.

Emotion-charged issues of previous teen generations sound like faint echoes of old rock records resurrected on FM stations. Gone are the generation-gap battles on—

- individuality versus conformity,
- freedom versus responsibility,
- doing your own thing versus doing the right thing.

The winding down of the Vietnam war and the end of the draft in the 1970s were the obvious turning points. On May 4, 1970, when Ohio national guardsmen opened fire on Kent State University students protesting the U.S. "incursion" into Cambodia, youthful emotions peaked. Students at 350 colleges went on strike, ROTC buildings on thirty campuses were burned, sixteen states called out the national guard.

Only three years later, when teacher-journalist Klaus Mehnert visited Kent State University, the fires were already going out among the young. He found that students who took him around "matter-of-factly pointed out where the national guardsmen stood and fired their shots, where the students were killed—much as if they were taking me over the field of Gettysburg or some other battleground of long ago."[6]

The year 1973 also brought the Arab oil embargo and the discovery of American vulnerability at the gas station. Young Americans became worried about losing their "wheels," symbols of their freedom. Instead of jeering, defiant young protesters, the TV screen showed high school students expressing not outrage but shock. World politics was reaching Main Street, and it threatened to "ground" them.

---

[6]Klaus Mehnert, *Twilight of Young* (New York: Holt, Rinehart & Winston, 1977), p. 37.

In the 1980s, rather than the effects of war and gas shortages, teenagers feel the impact of economic uncertainty and nuclear threats. These concerns are reflected in their outlook toward life. Teenagers are worried about the future of the world as well as their own future. Although they do not mount podiums, they do feel fragile and even worry about whether they and the world will survive. This was brought out pointedly when the World Future Society met in 1982 and various participants expressed their concern about the sense of futility among many young people.

Economic uncertainty has had a similar impact. The young do not argue supply-side economics, tax cuts, and budget deficits to express such a concern. They worry about getting a job and finding a place in American society. This shows up in a backing away from risk taking and a tendency to play it safe.

In commenting on a Carnegie Foundation study of U.S. college students, senior fellow Arthur Levine reported "a sense among today's undergraduates that they are passengers on a sinking ship, a *Titanic* if you will." In Iowa, the director of admissions at St. Ambrose College, James Barry, reported to *Time* magazine that "the good old days" of militant youth "never happened to them. . . . They hardly even talk about the 70s. It's just now. And now isn't so hot." Sociologist Jonathan Cole, who graduated from Columbia University in 1964 and now teaches there, offered a succinct retrospective: "We had a feeling then that the universe was expanding. Now these kids seem to feel it's contracting, closing in on them."

The uncertain generation has replaced the rebellious generation. As revolutionaries, American teenagers did not worry about making a living in a land of bigger and bigger. *Work,* yippie Abbie Hoffman announced, had become to young Americans "the only dirty four-letter word in the English language." Today, almost eight out of ten teenagers think they will achieve what they want in life by working for it.[7]

---

[7]Norman and Harris, *Private Life,* p. 291.

A Teenage Profile

An updated profile of today's teenagers must also deal with their greater sexual freedom, a trend that was dramatized by the revolutionary sixties but hardly created by it. It still goes on as the proportion of teenagers calling for greater sexual freedom increases from Gallup poll to Gallup poll: 48 percent in 1978, 53 percent in 1981.

Opinions aside, sexual behavior is indisputably freer. For example, the survey of 160,000 teenagers found that—

- almost six out of ten between the ages of sixteen and eighteen have had sexual intercourse,
- almost one of three between the ages of thirteen and fifteen have had sexual intercourse,
- the average age for first sexual experience is between fifteen and seventeen.[8]

At the same time—and this will surprise at least some parents—traditional values are becoming more appealing to teenagers. A May 1981 Gallup youth survey found that almost nine out of ten teenagers say they would welcome "more authority." Almost as high a proportion—85 percent—would welcome more family ties.

Other Gallup findings contribute to a teenage profile, reflecting increasingly strong support for more technology (85 percent), more self-expression (84 percent), less emphasis on money (68 percent), and more sexual freedom (53 percent). Only 31 percent would welcome less emphasis on work, and only 20 percent favored more marijuana acceptance (compared with 24 percent in 1978).

Gallup also found that only 43 percent of teenagers considered religious beliefs "very important" in their lives. Churchgoing dropped sharply between 1961 and 1981: from seven in ten attending church in a typical week to five in ten. Church membership dropped from eight in ten to seven in ten. However, even this picture may be too bleak, since the annual survey of incoming college freshmen by

---

[8]Ibid., p. 42.

16

the American Council on Education-UCLA found a different trend. In a survey of 1978 freshmen, 85 percent said they had attended church within the past year compared with 64 percent in 1966. That does not necessarily mean an increase in regular churchgoing, but it does point to continued contact with organized religion.

The profile makes sense when the concept of "deauthorization" is applied to the trends among teenagers. They do not automatically obey established authority, no doubt a trend accelerated by the revolutionary sixties and such national scandals as the Watergate cover-up. Something has been added to the natural teenage tendency to rebel: mistrust of established authority and readiness to feel justified in doubting, questioning, and even rejecting authority.

Dr. Saul Brown, director of the department of psychiatry at Cedars-Sinai Medical Center in Los Angeles, is emphatic on this point: "Teenagers have grown up on Watergate, and they feel those in power are out for themselves. Many seem to feel, 'Let me get what I can now!'"

Other observers have picked up on the theme of self-centeredness. The director of Massachusetts' Bureau of Student Services, Joan Schuman, has stated that the selfishness of teenagers strikes her "most of all," adding: "The predominant theme is 'What's in it for me?' and 'I don't care what happens to my fellow man.'" Atlanta psychiatrist Alfred Messer has noted: "The 'me' attitudes of many adults are now filtering down to lower age groups. Teenagers don't have enough good ego models." Psychology Professor Harry Schumer of the University of Massachusetts has struck a similar note: "They are returning to private goals. What matters is the here and now."

In our own contacts with parents and teachers, we have found that their primary concerns about teenagers fall into three major areas.

1. *Values.* Many teenagers are not developing strong commitments. In the sixties, teenagers were committed to causes, to direct action, to acting out. In the eighties, teenagers seem uncommitted, often withdrawn, sometimes indifferent.

2. *Lack of vision.* Teenagers are not only exhibiting confusion about who they are but seem to lack confidence that they can ever figure out "what life is all about." Their horizons seem to have shrunk.

3. *Religious indifference.* Parents who feel that organized religion is important find that teenage sons and daughters are complacent about religion. Religion does not loom as the place to turn when major issues confront them.

The findings culled from all these surveys and observers of the teenage scene may help to win an argument, but they do not promote meaningful dialogue between the generations. Succinct summaries of an entire generation land with a dull thud when dealing with flesh-and-blood teenagers. As we have already noted, summing up a generation is useful only if handled with care and with qualification.

With all these drawbacks, however, there are some benefits to be gained from an awareness of the generalizations being made about teenagers. We would like to single out three such benefits.

1. *Perspective.* In the heat of teen crisis and turbulence, both parents and their sons and daughters can lose perspective. Although each situation and each teenager is unique, there are points that all situations and all teenagers share in common.

2. *Understanding.* Reminders of what teenagers are going through can make it easier to establish contact with them, particularly when we realize how vulnerable and susceptible they are.

3. *Openness.* Listening, a theme which will recur in this book, depends on looking into the other person's world and on seeing things from his or her viewpoint.

In looking at teenagers today, there is a gloomy extreme arising from the alarming statistics about teenage suicide. "Suicides in this age group are probably the highest they have been in history," reports Dr. Derek Miller, chief of the Adolescent Program at Northwestern University's Institute of Psychiatry in Chicago. He estimates that there are five times as many suicides as are actually reported (official figures show five thousand annually) and "ten times as many suicide attempts as completed acts."[9] According to this estimate, suicide may very well be the leading cause of death among adolescents.

Dr. Miller cites a constellation of problems that undermine all teenagers, not only the suicidal: high divorce rate, breakdown of the extended family, lack of social ties, mobility, and availability of drugs. All these factors surround adolescence, making it "a time of enormous stress and turmoil."

But most parents will testify that teenagers, for all the toil and trouble, are making it through a difficult time of life during a difficult period in American society. These parents are seconded by a major study of some twenty thousand high school students in both public and Catholic schools. The survey is based on a cross section of students and presents a teenage psychological self-portrait. The results contradict the doom-and-gloom view of teenagers: "The vast majority of adolescents studied stated that they are happy, strong, and self-confident. The adolescents do not feel inferior to others, including their peers, and they do not feel that others treat them adversely."[10]

Based on our experiences with teenagers, parents, and teachers, we find that life with teenagers is lived between the extremes of suicide and tranquility. There are ups and downs in the lives of teenagers and there are questions, issues, and problems that parents and educators want to address. Just as teenagers face challenges, so do adults in relationship with them. On the whole, the encounter is demanding, energizing, and rewarding—also open-ended.

In this context, Erik H. Erikson, who has examined human development so thoroughly, makes this poignant observation:

---

[9]*Dallas Times Herald,* June 5, 1982.
[10]Daniel Offer, Eric Ostrov, Kenneth I. Howard, *The Adolescent: A Psychological Self-Portrait* (New York: Basic Books, 1981), p. 46.

For if the simplest moral rule is not to do to another what you would not wish to have done to you, the ethical rule of adulthood is to do to others what will help them, even as it helps you, to grow.[11]

IN A NUTSHELL

From yesterday's teenagers waving banners of protest to today's teenagers hunched over Pac-Man, the teenage image has switched from active to passive. Teenagers have gone out of the spotlight, but they are still living through the most turbulent part of their lives as they make the demanding, exciting, frustrating, fulfilling transition to adulthood.

Teenagers face a twofold challenge: the explosive teenage experience that is always there and the set of pressures and influences that arise from the particular times in which they live. Some things are changing, while the fundamental aspects of growing up remain the same. As in the past, teenagers are susceptible and vulnerable. Adults watching the current generation center their concerns about teenagers on values, on lack of vision, on religious indifference. For parents and teachers, the goal remains constant: to help teenagers grow into responsible, mature, fulfilled individuals. The big question, and the one underlying this book, is *how.*

---

[11]Erik H. Erikson, "Reflections on Dr. Borg's Life Cycle," in *Adulthood,* ed. Erik H. Erikson (New York: W. W. Norton & Co., 1978), p. 11.

DISCUSSION EXTENDERS

1. Would you like to be a teenager today? If you were, what would be your greatest joys? Your greatest problems?

2. How would you compare your answers to the first question with those of your teenage children?

3. What do you think of the music and movies that today's teenagers like? What do you think of their heroes?

4. What are some of the positive interests of the teenagers you know? What turns them off?

5. What worries teenagers today? Do they have reason to worry? How can parents and teachers respond to those worries?

6. What questions would you like to ask teenagers? What do you think their answers would be? (Try testing your answers against what teenagers themselves say.)

7. Do you make a conscientious effort to communicate with your teenage children about their problems and concerns? What could you do to improve communication with them?

8. What kinds of messages are communicated in your home through nonverbal language? What impact do these messages have?

9. How do your teenagers handle peer pressure? In what areas do they respond most to outside pressures?

10. What evidence do you see that "traditional values are becoming more appealing to teenagers"?

CHAPTER 2

What Do They Want?

Teenagers in the 1980s give the impression that they live in their own world of paradox. They may talk and act in ways that look traditional, but they don't take traditional answers for granted. They are ready to listen to parents and teachers, but they don't seem particularly impressed by what they hear. They accept the standard formula of good grades, hard work, and getting ready for a career, but apparently without enthusiasm. They seem to break rules without gusto and to conform without conviction.

Belief for today's teenagers does not come as easily as it did for the teenagers of either the conformist fifties or the rebellious sixties. Yesterday's teenagers conformed or rebelled with enthusiasm and/or conviction. What is often overlooked in regard to the rebels of the sixties is how automatic and unquestioning their attitudes were. They looked at the world in simplistic terms of good guy/bad guy and had no trouble identifying who was what. They might even have been more conformist than their con-forming predecessors, but it was their brand of conformity that upset parents and teachers.

If yesterday's teenagers said to parents, "We don't want what you want," today's teenagers would say, "We have to settle for what you want. What else is there?" At that level of response, teenagers are accepting the traditional goals of job and family. Interpretations of this response vary. Some argue that it shows teenagers to be more passive; others, that they are less gullible. On the negative side, teenagers are seen as apathetic, withdrawn, uninvolved; on the positive side, as self-contained, serious, sensible.

Teenagers have always confused their parents and teachers because they are sorting out their lives. But in the current context, they are confounding parents and teachers in a different way. Teenagers are hanging back, questioning, wondering what it all means to them. Their style seems uncertain, their mood tentative.

Today's teenagers reflect a national mood. Americans no longer take it for granted that each generation is going to be better off. The old conviction that "our kids will have it better" was rooted in immigrant dreams and was reinforced with each succeeding generation in the twentieth century. The post-World War II generation of parents had no doubt about it and thus were particularly vulnerable when their children in the sixties rejected their definition of "having it better."

Rising expectations now have given way to feelings of vulnerability among both parents and teenagers, particularly economic vulnerability. This is especially apparent when college-educated parents discuss college for their own sons and daughters. "Here I have worked hard and have gotten ahead," they will say, "but I can't afford to send my own child to the same college I went to." Among teenagers whose fathers have been fired from jobs, feelings of vulnerability are strongest. Not only do the next rungs on the ladder of upward mobility seem to be missing, but the ladder seems to have been taken away. Even with economic recovery, the scars shape and influence teenage perspectives, just as prosperous businessmen never forgot their childhood in the Great Depression.

In this context, what today's teenagers want is shaped by the conflict they feel between idealism and realism. This conflict influences their reactions, their views, and their plans for the future. Teenagers do not reject idealism, but on the other hand they are determined to be realistic.

24

On the whole, today's teenagers do not seem eager to apply Senator Edward Kennedy's description of his brother Robert to their own lives: Whereas some people see things as they are and ask, "Why?" there are those who dream things that never were and ask, "Why not?" Rather than seeking to change the world, teenagers appear focused on what they can do about themselves. (Words like *seem* and *appear* crop up in our discussion to emphasize that we are identifying patterns, not pigeonholing all teenagers.)

Realism Teen-style

Realism emerges in teenagers' sense of limitations—for their own efforts, values, goals, and dreams and for the efforts of those trying to change the world. Talking to students makes this clear (the brighter the students the clearer). In discussions of how to behave when faced with difficult choices, teenagers time and again say: "That's a beautiful way to go and it would be great if people could live that way. But that's not the way things really are." In earlier years, they would have scorned such an attitude as "selling out." Today, they may still see it as a form of selling out but take the view that they are being realistic.

"To be an idealistic person today," teenagers tell you, "is to just ask to be 'shut down.'" They look around at the world that is presented to them and tell you bluntly that what they see shows that "nice guys finish last." By *nice guys,* they mean "turn-the-other-cheek idealists."

In the self-portrait of twenty thousand teenagers, this attitude was evident when today's teenagers were asked to endorse various statements reflecting their view of society. Only 40 percent would endorse the statement "'Eye for an eye and tooth for a tooth' does not apply to our society." By contrast, in the early 1960s, 67 percent endorsed the statement.[1]

The news from everywhere dampens tendencies to get carried away by ideals or by leaders. Content analysis of the media is not needed to support the point that both

[1]Offer et al., *The Adolescent,* p. 165.

entertainment and news dramatize crisis and crime, corruption and scandal, revolution and war. Of course, each generation rediscovers sin, but for the current generation it is not accompanied by a chant of "We Shall Overcome." The mood is more like "We'll Make It . . . I Think."

The romanticism of the Camelot era of J. F. Kennedy is just that for today's teenagers—legendary. Hero after hero has suffered de-mythologizing, including the once-sainted President Kennedy, not to mention FDR. In a mass-media society where leaders are glorified, debunking is bound to produce shock and cynical reactions.

By the 1980s, teenagers had become skeptical of political and business leaders. A 1982 Gallup polling of teenagers showed the extent of their distrust. Only about one-third thought senators and congressmen have either high or very high ethical standards (36 percent for senators, 35 percent for congressmen). Only 31 percent thought that is the case for journalists, 27 percent for business executives. Among students sixteen to eighteen years old, suspicion increased: only 30 percent gave politicians high or very high ethical ratings, and only 25 percent gave such a rating to business executives. Moreover, the better the students, the more distrusting of congressmen and senators.

Economically, as well as politically, teenagers have been shocked. After all, they have been brought up to believe in consumption as their duty as Americans. Even through the rebellious sixties as teenagers denounced the "system," they held on to sports cars and expensive stereo equipment and records. They didn't worry about money then, but hard times in the eighties have made them worry.

Teenagers now tend to view the mass of other teenagers as competitors rather than as fellow allies in a cause. Today when students cheat on an exam, it is not defiance of the system but part of fighting for a place in it. More than half (55 percent) of the teenagers in one survey admitted that they cheat. As for studying, 60 percent said they do it only to pass an exam, not to learn.[2]

---

[2]Jane Norman and Myron W. Harris, *The Private Life of the American Teenager* (New York: Rawson, Wade Publishers, 1981), p. 126.

The practical side of education has become increasingly important to teenagers, as is evident among incoming college freshmen. When the college class of 1982 entered as freshmen, 60 percent openly identified making more money as an important reason to go to college. Said the dean of students at Columbia University, Roger Lehecka: "These young people feel they must make career decisions immediately or be left out. This element of panic is unhealthy. They're making premature decisions." Or, as echoed by a student in Texas studying agricultural economics: "You have to look at what kind of return you're going to get for your investment. You can't be a music major. It won't pay the bills."

This concern about financial security can make teenagers insensitive to social issues and the struggle of the disadvantaged. The affluence that bred passionate support of liberal causes has been replaced by economic worries that breed indifference to the plight of others. Teenagers are worried about themselves and their future. In that frame of mind, it is hard for them to worry about others.

Teen reactions can be curiously low-keyed. Their sense of outrage can come across as muted. Some even seem unable to react. In recent years, this has been dramatized for one of us (Father DiGiacomo) by what happens when high school students engage in a Socratic dialogue about values and conscience in conflict with authority. The goal of such dialogues is to help teenagers develop a moral style based on principle and personal conviction rather than on blind obedience, peer pressure, or selfishness.

One revealing dialogue centers around the My Lai massacre in Vietnam. The students first view a film documenting the horrors of Nazi concentration camps. At the end of the film the narrator comments that "the monster is still alive, and in our midst." Then, in another disturbing documentary, five Army veterans recount My Lai and bear witness to the needless slaughter of helpless villagers. In chilling rationalizations, one particular GI repeatedly refers to the need to obey orders without question. The "monster" of blind obedience to evil becomes evident as some teenagers point out they might have been in the same position.

27

Or if those GIs had never gone to war, they would have led normal lives, free of violence and savagery. Although some students are outraged at My Lai and demonstrate awareness of the evil involved, there are others who are caught up in nationalistic bias and still others who hardly react at all.

The absence of feelings and reactions is disturbing and indicative. Too many teenagers have trouble answering questions about how they feel. They prefer to say what they think rather than express what they feel. This is a change from one extreme to the other—from a previous generation that seemed to overreact to one that seems to underreact. Such extremes distort the reality of the inner lives of teenagers, but they do underline a difference at work in adult-teenage communications.

In his survey of twenty thousand teenagers, Dr. Daniel Offer, a psychiatrist renowned for his research among adolescents, found the same tendencies in comparing teenagers of the early 1960s with those of today. He found indications that the former had "somewhat more stable and well-structured ethical standards" and that the latter "have turned more inward and have a greater concern for themselves and less for their social environment." He also noted: "The teenagers in the early 1960s more often created an impression that they felt that the world was an exciting place, and they exhibited a certain amount of flair or élan that is lacking in today's teenagers."[3]

When teenagers talk of their own plans and aims, the same muted tones are evident. They want to work hard and get ahead, but they also make it clear that material success is not enough. Such success is tangible and measureable, but teenagers do not equate it with happiness, in spite of all the programming they have had to become consumers. They view the quality of the personal relationships in their lives as crucial. They realize that no amount of conspicuous consumption can substitute for love and friendship. Hence they decry materialism and long for something more, which brings us to the subject of idealism.

---

[3]Offer et al., *The Adolescent*, pp. 56, 57, 76.

Teenage Idealism

The idealism of the current generation of teenagers centers on relationships with others, a natural outgrowth of their absorption in peers and a carryover influence of the counterculture of the 1960s. Friendship and other people in their lives predominate in their outlook. Their realism says that the Golden Rule gets in the way; their idealism says that the Golden Rule is the way to live a satisfying life.

This ambivalence is reflected in teenage attitudes toward religion. On one hand, according to one survey, teenagers are less likely than adults to feel that religion is relevant today, and almost half feel that religion is losing its influence on American life. On the other hand, 57 percent of the teenagers responding to another survey felt that religion can answer all or most of today's problems. Only one-third viewed religion as outmoded. Skeptical attitudes were stronger among white teenagers, those with college-educated parents, those living in the East and Far West, and those who are Catholics.[4]

At the same time, a survey of 160,000 teenagers found that more than half (53 percent) planned to follow their parents' religion and one-fourth were "not sure." Only 15 percent answered with an outright "no." One sixteen-year-old Catholic summed up the spirit of independence that is increasingly common among Catholic teenagers: "I wouldn't change my religion, but I think women should be priests and I think the Catholic view about some TV shows is ridiculous. No church should tell you what you can or can't watch. I'm very anti on some of the things the church teaches, and I only go to Mass to please my mother. I don't go to Confession. Like I don't think telling a priest is going to make anything better. Just tell God you're sorry. The church doesn't like it and they say you shouldn't argue. But it's there to question, and I question my religion."[5]

---

[4]*Emerging Trends,* Princeton (New Jersey) Religious Research Center, October and March 1981.
[5]Norman and Harris, *Private Life,* p. 266.

A Quest for Meaning

Along with independence (an increasingly stronger ideal among teenagers) there is an openness to mystery, to the sacred, to the religious dimension of existence. This is apparent among those of us who spend much time talking seriously with today's young about their values, their hopes and dreams, and their search for meaning and satisfaction in their lives.

But this openness does not mean that teenagers are going to walk through the church door. The problem of getting them to church is greater than ever. More and more, their thrust toward independence makes them suspicious of conventional religion and hesitant about organized churches. They tend to want their religion "straight," and they readily pick up signs of unrest and criticism within Christendom.

Their idealism makes teenagers—quite rightly—insist that religion should make a difference in the way people live and treat one another. They are impatient with religious formalism of all kinds; they dismiss Sunday morning religion as hypocritical and, worse, pointless. Prayer and worship which have no discernible impact on people's values and life-styles strike them as more hypocrisy.

Because teenagers see the world in black and white, they readily conclude that religion which "does nothing for me" is worthless. "If I don't get anything out of Sunday worship, why should I go?" "If my local parish is filled with hypocrites, why should I let them infect me with their hypocrisy?" "If this is what religion is all about, then I'll take chocolate ice cream."

Still, there are strong signs that teenagers have not turned their backs on religion. More than that, there are signs of a strong yearning for meaning in life—a yearning no doubt intensified by fears about the world destroying itself. Rather than being closed off from religion, teenagers are often disappointed by organized religion. They want to experience religion—in the warmth and friendship of worship, in spontaneity and informality. What they don't experience, they don't feel. What they don't feel, they don't embrace.

Teenagers worry about the lack of values, direction, integrity, and religious faith—just as adults do—but in their own way. Their concern is less reflexive, less analytical. The same vacuum in values observed by commentators on the social scene is experienced by the young. Teenagers are trying to figure out what to do with their lives and are yearning for meaning in life itself. They do not necessarily use the same words, but they are definitely immersed in that process.

Realistically, teenagers recognize their immersion in materialism and the consumer society; idealistically, they sense that there is much more to life. The cult phenomenon has demonstrated how great that yearning becomes among the young by filling a religious vacuum.

A Minneapolis rabbi, Maurice Davis, has pinpointed the appeal of the cults with their offer of involvement, support, and a sense of belonging. He cites the "longing for an emotional relationship and satisfaction," something teenagers who join cults find nowhere else. One young man said flatly during deprogramming from a cult: "What I believed [in the cult] may have been nonsense, but at least I was believing. My parents believe in nothing."

Here is a significant answer to the question of what teenagers want. They want to believe. That desire runs through their idealism. It crashes against the rocks of teen realism, with differing results. Some turn away from religion disillusioned; others leap blindly into cults. In between, teenagers turn increasingly to Bible study and individualized opportunities to pray and to worship wherever they find themselves "at home."

Bible study has increased sharply. A Gallup youth survey has found that the proportion of teenagers participating in Bible study groups rose from 27 percent in 1978 to 41 percent in 1981. Even one-fifth of those teenagers who do not attend church were involved in Bible study groups. A study of 1982 college graduates reported that three out of ten described themselves as born-again Christians.

The current mood is distinctly different. The sixties were characterized by the rush to change the world in secular, humanist terms. The seventies were characterized as a "me" decade in which the young turned inward and meditation captured attention. In the eighties, teenagers are much more open to the questions of ultimate meaning seen in religious terms.

Cult leaders succeed by exploiting this craving for meaning. They have an advantage over those who speak for authentic religion. To young people who reject the constricted materialistic vision of the world and look for larger meaning, the cultist offers simplistic answers to complex questions, total security through the surrender of personal responsibility, and an immediate identity available without struggle or pain. The cults capture the young in a frozen time frame. They relieve them of the toil and trouble of growing up.

Authentic religion does not offer such an easy way out. It does not compromise with the mature commitment to live in the real world and to become involved with fellow believers in a community of belief without surrendering individual identity. Of course, parents and teachers would violate their own sense of self and of responsibility by responding to cults along the same lines of manipulation, distortion, and brainwashing. But adult believers can and should emulate the cults in offering involvement, support, and a sense of belonging to the young.

A Place in Society

This question of what teenagers want has to be faced within the context of their stage of development. At what is called the *conventional* level of moral development, teenagers are conformers, conforming to those in authority and to what they say is right and proper. The authority figures of parents and teachers are soon replaced by fellow teenagers and the surrogate authorities in the mass media, including celebrities and rock stars. Teenagers are looking around to see what they are supposed to do. Loyalty and obedience run strong. As much as they proclaim their independence, teenagers are deeply involved in one form of dependence or another.

32

Coming into their own as persons and adults means that teenagers develop their own identity, values, goals, and way of living. But before they get to that stage—and many adults don't reach that stage—teenagers rely on authority figures that they can respect and can listen to. Part of teenage tension today is the conflict between needing and mistrusting authority.

Parents enter into teenagers' lives by standing for certain values, standards, and goals, and then by feeling secure enough to defend them. This does not mean stifling or crushing teen independence. It means presenting a role model of an adult who has a sense of self and who has reached an autonomous stage of morality that does not depend on outside forces. Teenagers want and appreciate such role models in their lives.

What today's teenagers want can be described as the result of a realism-idealism accommodation. They are not going overboard in either direction. They seem to bring the notion of paradox into their attitudes and lives. In speaking of their attitudes toward patriotism, poet Allen Ginsberg has made the perceptive observation that "young people today are not unwilling to die for their country, but are simply unwilling to kill for it."

This attitude can be extended into many areas of teenage life.

- Teenagers want to be a success, but they don't want to make success the be-all and end-all.
- They want to get married and raise a family, but they don't want to be trapped in an unsuccessful marriage.
- They want to be moral and responsible, but they don't want to lose out to the immoral and the irresponsible.
- They want to "play the game," but they don't want to lose sight of right and wrong.
- They want to be accepted and liked by their friends, but they don't want to lose their individuality.
- They want to find meaning in religion, but they don't want to belong to a church just because "that's the thing to do."

33

Teenagers today live in irony as well as paradox. The irony is that teenagers have achieved what was demanded and struggled for in the sixties. They are taken seriously, listened to, given greater freedom. But they don't seem to be enjoying the fruits of such a victory. They are discovering that there are no shortcuts to growing up. The age-old challenge remains: to find out who we are and why we are here, and to decide what we are going to do. Today's teenagers reject easy and automatic answers to these questions. They apply their own particular mixture of idealism and realism and respond that they want to take their place in society and live both the good life and a meaningful life.

IN A NUTSHELL

Today's teenagers have an uncertain style and a tentative mood. They seem to embody a paradoxical mixture of realism and idealism as they try to figure out the world and their future place in it. They seem less imbued with the hope or expectation of changing the world and more concerned about making their way in it. They also seem to lack enthusiasm about how things will turn out. They sound and act as if they are ready to settle now for the best of whatever is available, not at all certain that it will satisfy them.

Their doubt about whether they will be satisfied with what the world will provide is a clear indication that teenagers sense there is much more in life than "making a buck." That's their idealism coming through. But at the same time they feel the need to find an economic niche for themselves. That's their realism. Thus teenagers are an enigma wrapped in hope and surrounded by uncertainty. They want a meaningful life as well as the good life, and they wonder whether the two can go together.

34

DISCUSSION EXTENDERS

1. What does it mean to be realistic? What do you think is the place of idealism in today's world?

2. What is your idea of a healthy balance between realism and idealism? How do you think your idea would differ from that of your teenagers?

3. Is there such a thing as a "free lunch"? If there isn't, what can we expect teenagers to do in order to "pay for their lunch"?

4. If you were a teenager today, what would your outlook on the future be like? How does that stack up against the outlook of teenagers you know?

5. How have your teenagers' views and their plans for the future been influenced by their sense of realism? By their sense of idealism? What are some things that add to their satisfaction with the world? To their dissatisfaction?

6. How do your teenage children express a yearning for meaning in life? What are they doing to satisfy that yearning? How are you helping them?

7. What were your own dreams as a teenager? Have you ever shared them with your teenage children? Are they interested?

8. Do we live in a society where the prevailing attitude is "an eye for an eye"? What examples can you give to illustrate your answer?

9. Do you expect your children to surpass your social and economic level? In comparison with other goals (such as "being happy," "helping others," "doing your own thing"), is "getting ahead" the most important?

10. What disappoints you most about the younger generation? What pleases you most? Do you ever share those views with your children? What are their reactions?

CHAPTER 3

E

nter the Parent

What do today's teenagers think about their rebellious predecessors of the 1960s?

For the past five years, one of us has made a practice of reading to his high school students the statements that his students made about religion and patriotism in the 1960s. Their reactions are revealing. They view their young ancestors as oddly fascinating, like citizens from some lost civilization. They find the statements overblown, simplistic, arrogant—which was often the case. They write their predecessors off as impractical extremists—once again, not far off the mark.

Yet there is a peculiar facet to this criticism. The students reject their predecessors' critique of traditional values and the social structures that embodied them not so much because they think the critique was invalid but because they view the attempts to change the status quo as impractical. Today's teenagers do not believe that the values and social structures that were attacked are all right but that it is futile to try to change them. Popular singer Billy Joel speaks for many in the song "Angry Young Man":

I believe I've passed the age of consciousness
    and righteous rage.
I've found that just surviving was a noble fight.
I once believed in causes too;
I had my pointless point of view,
And life went on no matter who was wrong
    or right.

Such apathy and resignation are not the qualities that we usually expect from American youth. We expect the young to have visions and dream dreams, and if their dreams are romantic and idealistic, so much the better. Such aspirations serve as a mechanism to protect a society from stagnation. And this is why the quiet conventionality of today's youth should not lull us into complacency. The quiet may not come from peace but from a vacuum.

Can adults do anything to fill that vacuum? They certainly can. But they can do so only within the context of the growing-up experience. That is, adults must face the fact that teenagers have entered a different stage of development and that they are getting their signals from a new and powerful source: their peers.

A brief flashback to childhood puts this teenage situation in perspective. Keep in mind that all human beings, young and old, have the fundamental need to feel that they are persons of worth, that they count for something.

From infancy, the sense of personal significance is picked up from signals given by other people. The infant who gets attention, whose curiosity is responded to, who is played with, is getting a supremely important message: *I am someone. I am lovable. People care about me and listen to me.* During the preschool years, when children want most of all to please their parents, signs of parental approval and encouragement help them build a positive self-image. In the early school years, when youngsters learn to interact with other children and develop mental, verbal, and social skills, the signals come from parent surrogates—called teachers.

All this time, children are uncritical conformists; they have to be. The world is too big and confusing for them to figure out by themselves, so they depend on trusted adults to show them the way. And all the significant others in their lives are probably telling them pretty much the same thing.

Peers Versus Parents

The situation usually begins to change during the early teen years. A powerful set of rivals—the peer group—challenges parents and teachers for the allegiance of these youngsters. Teenagers have an overwhelming need to be accepted by their contemporaries. As they take their first tentative steps out of childhood toward adulthood, it is not enough to be affirmed by their elders; in fact, such approbation may be seen as a liability, an embarrassment. For several years, they will often feel pulled in opposing directions. On the one hand, the love and approval of parents are still supremely important to them. On the other hand, they do not want to be left behind as more daring peers try to break away. And here is born a paradox familiar to anyone who has raised or worked with adolescents. They want to be free, to be out from under, to be on their own; yet they are terrified of seeming different, of appearing anything other than "normal," and of failing to blend into the protective foliage of the group.

Teenagers think of freedom in terms of being free *from.* They long for the day when adults will no longer be able to tell them when to come home, what to wear, where they may go. They do not understand freedom *for:* ability to act independently on interiorized values and self-chosen principles. They lack the ego strength needed to stand alone and resist peer pressure. This makes the teen years a volatile period. While teenagers are unable to take responsibility for themselves and their actions, they resist adult efforts to control them. For all their talk of freedom, they are not yet ready for it. If they do not conform to the adult establishment, they will conform to the leaders among their peers.

Faced with these conflicting pressures, adolescents have three choices. First, they can turn off their peers and devote themselves totally to satisfying the important adults and authority figures in their lives. At an extreme, teenagers who make this choice exhibit all the characteristics of the authoritarian personality—submissive, rigid, repressed. Second, they can reject the adult establishment and go all the way with the peer group. The late sixties, with the generation gap and the campus rebellions, were a spectacular example of such behavior. The third choice is the one most often made: to compromise and try to please everyone. This entails trying to satisfy different groups of people with quite different sets of expectations.

Teenagers who choose this third way feel obliged to live up to roles imposed by parents, teachers, peers, advertisers, and others. To keep hassles at a minimum, they may find themselves talking one way to their parents, another way to their friends, and still another way to their teachers— even about the same things. Putting on these masks and playing different roles can sometimes be so confusing that they end up wondering: *Who is the real me? Will the real me please stand up?* When this identity confusion is prolonged and unresolved, it becomes a major obstacle to maturity. (It also leaves young adults extremely vulnerable to manipulation and the quick fix of cults, as noted in the previous chapter.)

Parents and Values

Parents of teenagers often feel as though they are losers in the struggle with the peers of their sons and daughters. Teachers share the sense of frustration. But it is important to remember that though peers are more likely to influence *behavior,* parents have much greater influence over *values.*

Adolescents are easily pressured by their peers to go along with the crowd, but this happens in the area of action rather than in the domain of fundamental attitudes. Here parents still carry enormous weight, whether for good or for bad. High school teachers observe this almost every day, especially when their classes discuss economic, social, or political subjects. Then the teenage Archie

Bunkers make their sweeping observations on the human condition in terms that would make teachers despair if they did not realize that the teenagers are parroting adult pronouncements made around last night's dinner table.

But if parents can pass on negativism and cynicism to their children, they can also hand on optimism and hope. Just as they can infect them with prejudice and bigotry, so can they communicate tolerance and a sense of justice. If parents believe that whole groups of people are basically selfish, lazy, and not to be trusted, then their children probably think so too. If teenagers are convinced that the only realistic policy in a dog-eat-dog world is to be sure to get theirs and to hell with everybody else, the conviction is homegrown. On the other hand, if parents are open and constructive with others and show compassion and concern, they are helping their children avoid retreat into a narrow, selfish style of life. In a world of reduced prospects, insecurity, and defensive tribalism, one of the best things that can happen to a teenager is to grow up in a home where adults swim against the tides of negativism and isolation.

There is no question here of looking at life through rose-colored glasses. We do not have to close our eyes to evil in order to have hope in ourselves and in the people around us. If we aspire to be Christians, we must emulate Jesus and try to share his view of things. He always saw things as they were and called them that way. He denounced evil and never pretended that people or things were better than they were. But he told us of a just and faithful Father who loves us, warts and all, who never gives up on us, and who will have the last word. If we believe Jesus, we could never be so hard on ourselves or on others, and we would never try to stop the world and get off. We would resist the temptation to retreat into our own little island and pull in the drawbridge after us. And our children could learn, from watching us, how to believe in life.

This kind of healthy influence over growing children is achieved more by deeds than by words. A family that is not turned in on itself but actively involved in community concerns is educating its children in powerful ways. When parents take an active role in church affairs, children are encouraged to see religious faith not as a burden imposed from without but as an active force that motivates people to care and serve.

Conversely, parents who expect children to learn such ideas in school or religious education classes without seeing them practiced at home are asking the impossible. Teachers cannot accomplish with words what parents do not confirm by deeds. Yet it is amazing how many parents expect religious educators to do that very thing. Parents want their children to learn honesty even though they chisel and cut corners and the kids know it. They want their children to go to church even though they themselves do not. They want their babies to be baptized when they have ceased to practice their faith. Not all the failures of religious education can be laid at parents' doors, but a great many can. "Do as I say, not as I do" is the self-defeating rule that is still around and always will be, with the same predictable results. Adults may charitably call it inconsistency. Teenagers have a harsher name: hypocrisy.

Peers and Behavior

Even as we acknowledge the crucial role of parents in the formation of teenagers' attitudes and values, we must address ourselves in practical terms to the impact of peers on behavior. For it is here that even the best parental influence and example can be undermined, sometimes with tragic results.

The first thing to observe is that peer influence is often good. Youngsters who have healthy attitudes toward school and who keep out of serious trouble usually gravitate toward like-minded companions and influence one another in positive ways. If your children have friends like that, you are indeed blessed. And if you can encourage these associations by offering their friends an unobtrusive welcome in your home, do so. If your sons or daughters make these friends by participating in high school activities or sports, grin and bear it if these activities occasionally make them late for dinner. If they are spending time with good companions in healthy pursuits, you are well ahead in the parenting game.

But you cannot always determine whether your children's friends are a good or a bad influence. One thing you should do is try to know who those friends are. This is easier to do when the children are younger, but as they enter the teens you must be careful not to seem too vigilant. The older they get, the more unwise it becomes to insist on knowing *what* they are doing, but it is not unreasonable to ask *where* and *with whom.* When you meet these friends, exercise caution in making judgments. Sometimes the sloppy, long-haired kid is harmless, while the polite, well-dressed one is doing the con job.

There are some danger signals to be alert to. If groups of kids suddenly fall silent at your approach, there is a possibility that they have something to hide. Don't jump to conclusions, but keep your eyes and ears open. Also watch out for companions who are two or three years older than your teenager. It is much harder to resist pressure from someone older than from someone the same age. And the older teenager may have a problem too, especially if he or she habitually hangs out with younger ones. Boy-girl friendships can be particularly troublesome if the age difference is too great. Since girls generally mature somewhat sooner than boys, it is natural for boys to date girls who are a bit younger. Some families make it a rule that no son or daughter may date anyone who is more than two or three years older or younger.

Many of these suggestions come from Dr. Victor B. Cline, who as a father of nine wrote *How to Make Your Child a Winner.* He wisely observes that parental interference in a teenager's social life is always risky and usually costly. But sometimes the association is so dangerous and the influence so destructive that strong measures are called for.

> Suppose . . . your kid is fifteen, and he hangs around with a group of juvenile delinquents who have got in trouble with the law several times. You know that he's no stranger to drugs, sex, and

petty crime. . . . It doesn't matter that your kid is basically good and sometimes a bit ashamed of the kind of things his friends do. He's with them, he's being influenced by them, and unless you do something *now* his whole future may be utterly ruined. . . .

This is not the time to be democratic. . . . It is not necessary to give him a vote. If he is young enough, simply forbid the friendship. Keep him home, drive him to and from school. . . . If he is too old or the friends are in school with him, take more drastic action. Change schools. Send him to live with relatives in a different state. . . .

If all else fails, you might seriously consider uprooting your entire family for the sake of that threatened child. Change jobs, move to a different state or to a different kind of neighborhood . . . do whatever you have to do to save your child's life.[1]

That's strong stuff. Fortunately, as Dr. Cline points out, most crises can be headed off before extreme measures are needed. But we must be prepared to face the fact that there are times when teenagers are simply unable to deal with pressure by themselves. Then it becomes irresponsible to leave them on their own.

Conflicting Messages

The pressures to conform do not come only from peers in school and neighborhood. The teenage need to be accepted is played upon by the media, especially by advertisers, movie producers, and TV programmers. Advertisers aim their messages at teens who want desperately to wear the right jeans, listen to the right music, and own the electronic equipment without which life could hardly go on.

---

[1]Victor B. Cline, *How to Make Your Child a Winner* (New York: Walker & Co., 1980), pp. 187-88.

Inexperienced young people are constantly receiving messages on how a woman or a man is supposed to act. These messages are shallow at best and corrupting at worst.

Sexuality is probably the most notorious area of conflicting expectations confronting adolescents. From parents, church, and teachers they hear that sex is serious, that intimacy is for people who are committed to and responsible for each other. They are told that premarital sex is wrong, that it can lead to venereal disease, pregnancy, unwanted children, or abortion. They are warned against getting involved in situations and relationships that are too heavy for them to handle at this point in their lives. From many of their friends, from television, movies, magazines, and music, they hear just the opposite: that fun sex is okay as long as nobody gets hurt; that if you really "love" someone, you don't need a piece of paper in order to go to bed with him or her. Teenagers are told that everyone is doing it, except creeps. *You don't want to be a creep, do you?* The message is insistent: the way to prove you are a man or a woman is by *performing;* if you're old enough to vote and still a virgin, you've got a problem.

Of course, young people are not the only ones subject to this pressure. Adults are under the gun, too, from a multibillion-dollar sex industry that must create a demand to keep pace with its supply. But teens are more vulnerable to manipulation because they are usually less able to deal with loneliness, rejection, and self-doubt. After all, if half the people they listen to say there is something wrong with them, teenagers cannot help wondering, at least, if maybe they are right.

The message of maturity becomes garbled. It does not come through clearly as parents strive to help teenagers develop a personal set of values and standards, a sense of self-worth, and the courage to act consistently with self-chosen ideals. Being mature means standing up to peer pressure and refusing to be intimidated. To do this in the America of the 1980s—especially in the matter of sexual attitudes, standards, and behavior—is difficult, even for adults. For adolescents, it is a real accomplishment. They

need help to see through false images and to become discriminating consumers of popular culture. It is hard for
teenagers to see clearly the consumerism and hedonism
that dominate much of their world because they are so
close to these influences. But their chances are improved
if their parents are clear in their own minds that people are
more important than things and if their parents' ambitions
go beyond conspicuous consumption and self-indulgence.

Vision and Values

As children grow up, there are other things to look for
besides their appearance, health, and achievements in
school. What is their idea of success? What is their vision
of the good life? What do they value? Why does your
daughter want to be a doctor—to heal or to get rich? Does
your son's ambition to study law have anything to do with
the pursuit of justice? Does the notion of service play any
part in your children's hopes and dreams? If you can discuss these things with them, you can get an idea of the
direction their conformity is taking them. If their ambitions are too limited, you may be able to open them up to a
world larger than the plastic paradise to which so many
aspire.

Teenage spending itself says a great deal. It indicates
what counts most for youngsters and reflects the influence
of teen society. Typically, their spending reveals the pressure to conform and to keep up with their peers. High
school teacher David Powell, a perceptive observer as well
as author, notes that "spending money is a way that teens
compete with one another." When he asks high school
girls how much they think should be spent on clothes,
makeup, and so on, he gets a startling response: $1,500 to
$2,000 a year. When asked how much they actually spend,
the girls answer: $1,000. Powell reports: "They feel they
should be spending more! They feel guilty because they
haven't spent as much as they *should*. The ads have brainwashed them."

Like the rest of us, teenagers are both targets and victims
of advertising bombardments. As one sociologist observed,

46

if Americans are trained from childhood to be consumers, a TV program like "The Price Is Right" is a postgraduate course in consumption. From their nursery-room exposure to television, American children go into lifelong training as consumers. Madison Avenue imposes an economic duty on them—to buy the latest. Obviously, parents need to look at themselves before leaping to criticize teenage spending. What kind of adult role models do teenagers have at home?

Psychologically, controlling their own money—as in controlling their own space—is part of growing up. It is a sign of independence and it calls for decision making. As a limited commodity, money demands that choices be made. Spending it one way prevents spending it another way. Once their money is spent, teenagers must then live with the consequences of their decisions. If parents bail them out of the consequences, they undermine the lesson. The other extreme—taking away the power to make spending decisions—deprives teenagers of an important learning experience.

When parents impose restrictions on spending, teenagers deserve to know in advance what they are. (Obviously, parents take for granted the obligation to prevent purchase of dangerous substances.) Imposing restrictions belatedly or condemning teen choices comes across as arbitrary. Teenagers may then feel double-crossed. They want to know: "Is it my money or isn't it?" What is often hard for parents to accept is the different set of choices that teenagers make. From one generation to the next, the object of consumption differs, but impulse buying, faddish purchasing, and spending splurges are part of a universal process. Oftentimes, parents must say to each other, "This too shall pass," and let teenagers follow their particular piper.

When teenagers start earning their own money regularly, they add a new dimension to their growing independence. What they earn they want to control. Here, individual personalities emerge. Some save; others splurge. Some see their earnings as helping the family finances; others see their earnings as separate from the family. Any sensible response takes into account family circumstances as well as individual differences among teenagers. What really counts is not what they do with their money but who they are.

Before parents can help their children, they need to sort out their own life view. Would they like their teenagers to go beyond conventionality someday and become nonconforming individuals? Parents need to consider the implications before answering the question for themselves. People who conform to the expectations of conventional society find acceptance, avoid conflict, and generally fit in. Nonconformists may experience conflict and rejection, part of the price for individuality. There are pluses and minuses in both life-styles. Conventional people have less excitement but more security; unconventional folks are open to more varied experience, but the road to fulfillment can be a lonely one.

Let us be clear on what is meant by *nonconformity.* It does not mean being outlandish or weird, striking bizarre poses in order to outrage less imaginative people. Exhibitionism is only surface nonconformity. You can wear a three-piece suit, read the *Wall Street Journal,* and catch the 8:04 from Scarsdale every morning and still be a nonconformist in the sense that we are talking about. Being a nonconformist means that you are a person of principle, that you choose your life rather than let others choose for you, that you try to live less by conventional wisdom than by your own deepest personal convictions about what is right and wrong, what is true and worthwhile and just. How does that sound to you—inspiring, or scary, or crazy? We are not talking about kids now. We are talking about grown-ups, which is what teenagers are going to be in a very few years.

Not everyone chooses his or her life. Many let others choose for them. They let the group, or the crowd, or "society" decide for them what is important, what is valuable, what is acceptable. There is a solid body of opinion among psychologists and social critics, as well as a good deal of supporting evidence, that most people fall into this second category. How would you honestly classify yourself? And which direction would you like to see your children take in their adult years?

If you are like most people and place a higher value on social acceptability than on personal autonomy, then you will not be troubled that your teenagers conform, but that they conform to the wrong standards or the wrong people. This is not an idle distinction. Although you cannot make your offspring turn out the way you want, your values and your world view do have an impact on them. If your bottom-line version of a good human being is one who obeys the rules blindly and goes along with conventional wisdom, you will judge your children's growth in one way. If, on the other hand, your ideal people are those who take responsibility for their existence and refuse to compromise their deepest personal convictions, you will use another yardstick. And your children will know the difference.

These two divergent life views have an impact in many important areas. Citizenship, education, career, and religion are all deeply affected. Conventional people equate responsible citizenship with unconditional loyalty to government and law; nonconformists will not rule out the possiblility of dissent, conscientious objection, and even civil disobedience as a matter of principle. The conventionals want schools to prepare young people to fit in, to find their place in the established order of things; individualists want education to promote critical thinking, to challenge and even change the status quo. Conformists will make career choices according to conventional standards of utility and success; nonconformists are more likely to make such decisions in terms of social consequences or personal satisfaction. Finally, conventional adults will gravitate toward a religious style and a church which stress obedience to authority and fidelity to tradition; nonconformists will set great store by personal conviction, personal experience, and freedom of conscience and expression.

All the above contrasts are oversimplified and call for more careful distinctions. But they do help parents dredge up and confront the hidden agenda that underlies the hopes, the fears, and the plans they have for their children.

Unearthing this agenda helps parents determine whether they really want their sons and daughters to go beyond conformity or simply to change that conformity's direction.

Does it make a difference which path you and your children choose? Does it really matter whether they opt for critical thinking and individuality or settle for a comfortable accommodation to conventional standards of values and behavior? Maybe they would be better off and would lead a more trouble-free existence if they tried to blend in and if they did not ask too many questions. There are no easy answers, but we get some hints if we know where to look.

Consider some events of recent history. At the Nuremberg trials following World War II, men and women who had committed genocide on a scale that we still find hard to comprehend defended their actions on the grounds that they were patriots and good soldiers who were just following orders. Twenty-five years later, Americans did not know what to do with Lieutenant William Calley when he justified his supervision of the My Lai massacre with the same rationalizations. Opponents of racial injustice like Martin Luther King, Jr., suffered more from the apathy of uncommitted people than from the open attacks of bigots. Watergate conspirators preached, in the self-justifying words of John Dean, that the way to get along is to go along. And in the face of an unremitting nuclear arms race, most people stand aside rather than stand against the madness that threatens us all with extinction.

The question each of us must answer for ourselves is this: What kind of people does the world need today? Would we all be better off if people stopped questioning the priorities and goals set by those who wield authority? Or do we need more people who will question the unquestionable, insist on answers that make sense, and refuse to abdicate responsibility for themselves and their world?

The Christian View

Does Christianity throw any light on all this? Well, organized religion has not usually been noted for speaking up against the established order of things, especially if it involves any risk. But there have been exceptions. The Vietnam War was the first armed conflict to arouse opposition from American churches. The latter were also prominent in the civil rights struggles of the sixties. And U.S. Catholic bishops are wrestling with their consciences as they try to provide moral leadership in a time of nuclear peril. In these situations the Christian churches resemble their founder, Jesus Christ. Whatever he was, he was not conventional. For insisting that people were more important than laws and for siding with the poor and the outcast against the rich and powerful, he got himself killed as a rabble-rouser. Is this the way he comes across from the pulpits and in Bible classes? Would you want your children to emulate him?

Religion has traditionally been valued and respected, even by the unchurched, because it contributes to order and stability. (In Latin America, where it threatens the status quo, it is treated more harshly.) Parochial schools are given high marks, even by their adversaries, for maintaining discipline and instilling good study and work habits—surely reasons to be proud of church-related education.

But there are also disturbing questions to face: Is this enough? Are the graduates of these schools distinguishable from other Americans in their values and aspirations? Are students taught to be critical of the destructive elements of our culture? Is it enough to be against abortion and communism and stop there when a host of other issues cries out for moral evaluation and response? Teenagers are limited in their ability to deal with these issues, but high school is a good place to begin. Later may be too late.

The Road to Maturity

By now, some readers must wonder: Are you guys serious? Don't you know that asking teenagers to engage in criticism and dissent is like throwing gasoline on a fire? Parents and teachers have their hands full getting teenagers to respect authority and to obey the rules laid down by society.

No, we are not against the solid virtues of obedience and respect for law and order. But remember what Pogo once said in the late Walt Kelly's comic strip: "We have met the enemy, and they are us." Elements in our culture and our institutions need to be criticized, even at times rejected. By the time children reach their teens, they can begin to learn how to separate wheat from chaff. But someone has to help them. Teachers attuned to teenage possibilities as well as limitations can engage students in a constructive critique of the forces that touch their lives. Teachers can counter the tendencies indicted by social philosopher Michael Novak:

> The treadmill on which our students are expected to take their place at graduation deadens criticism and creativity. American culture governs American schools; . . . the same climb to success, the same petty prejudices, the same imperceptive attitudes mark the campuses as mark the businesses and professions in the towns. The [schools] . . . turn students back to their home towns with nearly the same prejudices, interests, and habits as they had when they came to school. The quality of political debate in America is so low, vulgar, and inadequate that one must question why education (as we now have it) is essential to democracy: What does it add to the natural man? Where are numbers of Americans . . . who read with discrimination? who understand *both* sides of an argument? . . . who have by habit the Socratic or religious passion for personal and social reform? Schools neglect the life of the Spirit at the peril of the entire culture.[2]

---

[2]Michael Novak, *A New Generation* (New York: Herder & Herder, 1964), p. 122 (slightly adapted by Michael Novak).

When parents encourage healthy skepticism and free inquiry at home, teenagers have a much greater chance of rising above the mediocrity of the unquestioning mob. Certainly risks are involved, but the stakes make them worthwhile. Taking risks is the road to responsible maturity—a rocky road, one with possible detours, but a road that respects the stakes in growing up, as eloquently set forth by Novak:

> Besides needing to do the world's work, they need to discover themselves. . . . More than they need to possess things, they need to come to know and appropriate themselves—to find themselves in the mazes of ignorance, passion, and self-illusion which hide them from themselves. They need to know that each of them is unique and irreplaceable, not for what he has or can do, . . . but for what he is. . . . Many are restless and discontent. In their eyes one can sometimes see a question difficult to voice: What have I lost? What turn in the road was a mistake? . . .
>
> To become a person is not easy. The task needs all the resources of education. Unless there are persons, moreover, faith in God is meaningless. The shallowness of American religion is largely due to the style of American education. Moreover, shallowness easily gives way to extremism, right or left. Sound judgment is a sign of integrity of spirit—being in touch with reality is the spirit's highest flowering.[3]

Conformism is not peculiar to adolescence. The challenge to become our own persons and to choose our lives rather than let others decide for us begins in youth and continues in adult life. To help teenagers meet the challenge, we must do more than oppose bad influences. We must play for higher stakes, aiming beyond bland conventionality toward the genuine self-determination of full

---

[3]Ibid., pp. 123-24 (slightly adapted by Michael Novak).

personhood. When schools explicitly aim at this goal and parents support such an effort at home, young people have powerful allies in the struggle to find themselves.

No one experienced in dealing with teenagers—as parent or teacher—underestimates the difficulty of this task. The degree of difficulty is illustrated by two experiences among countless examples encountered in high school religion classes by one of the authors.

In the first example, a class of juniors was discussing the case of Pontius Pilate and his condemnation of Jesus. The discussion centered on the guilt of the Roman governor who refused to exonerate the defendant after admitting that none of the charges had been proven. The verdict of several students was that Pilate wasn't guilty of anything! Why? "Because he was under pressure! After all, he had to keep the peace too, and releasing the prisoner might have caused trouble. Besides, he might have a family to support, and losing the governor's job could be a big problem." No exaggeration; that's what they said.

The second example comes from a freshmen class that was discussing the story of Zacchaeus, the man inspired by Jesus to stop ripping off people and to give back the money he had stolen. Some students expressed the opinion that Zacchaeus would have been better off if he had never met Jesus. Why? "Because before he met Jesus, he was rich and could provide many things for his family; after his conversion, he lost a lot of money and was poor."

But we should not be too surprised. After all, the teenagers were just saying out loud what many Americans believe deep down—that honesty and justice are good, except when they cost you money.

Can teenagers do better than this? Obviously, there is no simple, foolproof formula, but a foundation can be built. People who cannot stand up against pressure—whether peer pressure or economic pressure—have an unconsciously low opinion of themselves. Without spelling it out for themselves, they think that if certain people reject them, they are worth nothing. They unwittingly accept the unspoken premise that you are what you own, that possessions bestow personhood, and that therefore every value is hostage to the dollar sign. What these people, young and old, need is the bedrock conviction that they are persons of worth, lovable and loved, regardless of how much they own or don't own, whether some people approve of them or not.

Where do they get this conviction? We come back full circle—to the home, within the family, where children learn at the very beginning of life that they are someone because parents love them, encourage them, discipline them, listen to them, worry about them, are proud of them. As they grow up, it is crucial that they perceive themselves as loved, not just for being handsome or smart or popular or athletic, but just for being who they are. This is the precious awareness of being *unconditionally* loved—no strings attached. This kind of love does not have to be earned; it is the kind that will not be withdrawn, no matter what.

Not all parents bestow this kind of love, the kind that can see a young person through the stresses and strains of adolescence and the thousand natural shocks that assault their self-esteem. Unconditional love is the kind of love that, Jesus says, God has for us. So if parents love their children that way, they are following God's example.

Just make sure teenagers know it.

They can take it from there.

IN A NUTSHELL

Today's teenagers are quieter and more manageable than their counterparts in the sixties. But, far from being satisfied with the world, they often seem to despair of changing it. Parents and other caring adults who wish to influence the young must cope with many competing forces, peer pressure most of all. Parents have less impact on their teenagers' behavior than on their values; parental influence can be good or bad, depending on the attitudes and values of the parents. Pressures to conform also come from mass media, whose pervasive messages often subvert parental values.

Teenagers need help to become individuals capable of resisting conformity in favor of integrity. But this can be threatening to parents who want their children to aspire only to safe conventionality. Recent history demonstrates the inadequacy of submissiveness and unquestioning loyalty. Even religion, often perceived as the guarantor of accepted behavior, must not only accept the risks of individuality but make a positive contribution to personal integrity. Young people need inner-directed parents who rise above mediocrity in their values, beliefs, and commitments, and who point the way to genuine maturity.

DISCUSSION EXTENDERS

1. Do you want your children to fit into society or to change it? Why?

2. What do you think is the place of personal conscience in the face of civil and religious authority?

3. Do your children reflect the values you want them to carry throughout their life? What can you do to instill these values so that they are not slaves to outside pressures?

4. How well are you acquainted with your teenagers' friends? What problems have you encountered in trying to keep track of what your teenagers are doing and with whom? What have you done to try to overcome these problems?

5. Have you had experiences of success or failure in dealing with peer pressure on your children? What were these experiences about, and how did you cope with them?

6. What are some of the false values presented by entertainment media? Can adults do anything to counteract their influence?

7. Are your children's schools teaching values like critical thinking and individuality, or are they reinforcing submissiveness and conventionality? What would you like them to do?

8. How is your teenagers' spending influenced by their peers? By media advertising? What restrictions on spending have you imposed? With what results?

9. How have you helped your teenage children meet the challenge of becoming their own person and choosing their own life? What role has your church played in helping them meet this challenge?

10. How do you try to get across to your children that they are unconditionally loved?

CHAPTER 4

Drugs: Who and Why

The lesson of American Prohibition is back a second time—this time with a teenage twist.

Prohibition did not and cannot work. American youngsters cannot and are not being kept away from alcohol and other drugs. Teenagers live in a smoke-filled world and go to parties where joints and alcoholic drinks are as standard as pretzels and potato chips.

When researchers Jane Norman and Myron W. Harris reported on their survey of 160,000 teenagers, they made the following comments after quoting two sixteen-year-olds who described alcohol and pot as part of their everyday environment.

> These are not the comments of a small or special sector of the teenage population. They are quotes from the average teenagers we interviewed in communities throughout the country. Girls, boys, athletes, students preparing for college. Whites, blacks, Protestants, Catholics, Jews.

The children of doctors, lawyers, and company presidents, and the children of factory workers, clerks, secretaries.

Our kids are getting high, and it's time we learned why and how directly from them.[1]

In our view, that is the appropriate starting point for a discussion of drugs, including alcohol—their prevalence. Parents who deny the facts about the prevalence of drugs are running from reality. Another flight from reality is pursued by parents who decide their children are addicts or alcoholics at the first sign of pot smoking or alcohol drinking. One extreme represents irresponsible escapism; the other, misguided alarmism. In both extremes, the emphasis is on *what* rather than on *who* and *why.*

The prevalence of drugs and drinking among teenagers is a sign of the times. The way in which teenagers deal with drugs and drinking is a symptom of what is going on in their growing-up years. They can hardly avoid decisions on drugs and drinking, and few opt for abstinence. The significant question is, What happens after they take that first drink or smoke that first joint?

Data on Alcohol and Pot

By the time youngsters reach high school, drinking is already part of their lives. As the National Council on Alcoholism reports:

- The average age for the first drink is thirteen.
- More than half of the youngsters in seventh grade have tried alcohol; by senior year of high school, nine out of ten have tried it.
- Teenage girls are drinking almost as much as boys (a new trend).
- Almost one out of five teenagers (19 percent) get drunk at least once a month.

---

[1]Jane Norman and Myron W. Harris, *The Private Life of the American Teenager* (New York: Rawson, Wade Publishers, 1981), p. 88.

- On the average, teenagers drink about five times a month.

The Norman-Harris survey of 160,000 young people found that one out of four high schoolers drinks more than once a week, even though three-fifths believe drinking is bad for their health.[2]

While drug use appears to have leveled off, it is still widespread. The annual 1980 sampling of high school seniors by the National Institute on Drug Abuse found that 65 percent said they had used drugs, an 18 percent increase over 1975. Moreover, almost two out of five (39 percent) tried drugs other than marijuana, largely because of the growing popularity of cocaine and other "uppers." While daily use of marijuana dropped by 12 percent between 1979 and 1980, nearly one out of ten high school seniors said they smoke it daily.[3] The Norman-Harris survey found that two out of five teenagers smoke marijuana regularly and that seven out of ten have tried it.[4] When the *New York Times* surveyed more than one thousand high school sophomores and juniors in city and suburban schools, it reported that "nearly all teenagers in the New York metropolitan region have come to regard illicit drugs as commonplace."[5]

For the most part, parents react differently to the use of pot and to drinking. The *New York Times* survey found parents more tolerant of drinking: only 1 percent of the students said their parents would not care if they (the students) smoked marijuana compared with 15 percent who said their parents would not care if they drank. The Norman-Harris survey found that the majority of the teenagers said their parents know they drink, but only 29 percent said their parents know they smoke pot. Fifty percent said they would lie to their parents about using pot, and more than half (55 percent) have never discussed the

[2]Ibid., p. 87.
[3]*New York Times,* February 19, 1981.
[4]Norman and Harris, *Private Life,* p. 87.
[5]*New York Times,* July 19, 1981.

taboo topic of drugs with their parents.[6] Some parents even admit they are "relieved" that their children are drinking rather than using drugs, thereby creating a more permissive atmosphere for drinking beer and wine—the most popular teenage alcoholic drinks.

There are even signs that parental permissiveness is extending to drugs. In addition, younger teachers, shaped by the counterculture, tend to be more tolerant as a result of being one-time or current pot smokers themselves. Even teenagers whose parents are dead set against any drugs are affected by greater adult permissiveness that is filtered through their friends and sometimes even through their teachers. This atmosphere was summed up by the director of a drug counseling program in the New York City schools, Naomi Barber.

> Ten years ago if a kid even mentioned marijuana his parents wanted to send him to reform school, you know, he was a drug addict, he was breaking the law. That was no good. But today a lot of adults think it's perfectly all right. The attitude that it's no worse than a drink has become popular.
>
> To try to talk to children about why drugs are not good for them in an atmosphere in which their parents can't see the problem and many have one themselves is difficult. In the last few years when I've talked to some of the younger teachers, some of them have also had the attitude of what's wrong with it.[7]

Which Is Worse?

Parental confusion on the issue of pot versus alcohol was expressed by a working mother who reported that her fifteen-year-old son swore off pot, promising that "he'll

---

[6]Norman and Harris, *Private Life,* p. 87.
[7]Quoted in *New York Times,* July 19, 1981.

never smoke it again." The mother said, "I want to believe him. He says he had a bad experience with pot, that it made him hallucinate, and that he'll never smoke it again. I hope he's telling me the truth. One thing worries me, though. The other night I found beer cans under his bed. Empties. So I guess he's drinking beer."

Then the mother put all her worries into a single question: "Which is worse for a fifteen-year-old: smoking pot or drinking beer?"[8]

This is a poignant example of how parents can focus on *what* rather than on *who* and *why*. Whether a teenager is taking drugs or drinking alcohol, he or she is using a drug— a mind-altering substance that can be hazardous. Abusing that drug is a sign that the individual has a problem. The main focus should be on that individual and the problem or problems.

Let us clear up some of the confusion about drugs by first considering what drugs are. Experts define a drug as any chemical that—

1. modifies the function of living tissues, resulting in physiological or behavioral change,
2. alters physical or psychological functioning,
3. alters an individual's physical, mental, emotional, or social condition.

In setting forth these definitions, two experts—Dr. Charles L. Whitfield and Mary T. Browning—point out that food, tea, coffee, and tobacco fall into this category. Then they add the significant dimension: the degree of hazard.[9] That is basically why parents worry about drugs. Caffeine may cause jitters, sweets may cause pimples, overeating leads to overweight. But drugs are dangerous; they can destroy.

---

[8]*Brooklyn Tablet,* September 18, 1982.
[9]Mary T. Browning and Charles L. Whitfield, "The Language and Literature of Alcoholism and Other Drug Problems," in *The Patient with Alcoholism and Other Drug Problems* by Charles L. Whitfield and Kenneth Williams (Privately printed, 1976), pp. 384-93.

Typically, parents and teenagers disagree on the dangers of drinking alcohol and of smoking pot. Alcohol, the parents' choice of drug, seems much less dangerous than marijuana, the teenagers' choice. Even the language of drugs sets the generations apart — *reefer, pot, grass, Mary Jane, smoke,* and *joint* for marijuana; *ludes* for the depressant Quaalude; *volumes* for Valium; *toot, coke,* and *snow* for cocaine. Family arguments wander off in the direction of "your" drug versus "my" drug, of legality versus illegality, of the difference between getting high on pot and getting high on alcohol. And so a confused and worried mother asks, "Which is worse for a fifteen-year-old: smoking pot or drinking beer?"

The dead end of such discussions is underlined by new alarms raised about teenage alcoholism. The media have proclaimed alcohol to be the latest teen drug, citing the estimates of the National Institute on Alcohol Abuse and Alcoholism (NIAAA). There are 3.3 million "problem drinkers" among teenagers — those who have had run-ins with police or teachers as a result of drinking. Added to this is the alarming statistic that alcohol-related car accidents are the number one killer of young people. One drug can be exchanged for another. The drug problem remains.

Here medical advice cuts through the debate: "Too often we focus more on the drug than on the individual with problems. Avoiding the drug is usually therapeutic, especially in the case of alcoholism, but understanding and coping with one's problems is the most therapeutic. Thus, drug dependency or misuse is merely a symptom or sign of a major underlying problem or a group of problems."[10]

In short, drugs provide a short-term solution and create medium- and long-term problems. As noted by Dr. Mitchell Rosenthal, president of Phoenix House, the nation's largest private residential drug-treatment program: "For young people, drugs are not used to enhance life. Drugs are used to go through life. Then the trap is set. The ominous signs

---

[10]Ibid., p. 386.

are there. We are going from the occasional to the dysfunctional. We are moving from parental self-medication and seeing its feedback among their children."[11]

The Danger Signs

Today, parents are at the point where the realistic question is not whether teenagers have tried alcohol and other drugs. The question is not *use,* but *abuse.* The concern is whether drugs are disrupting the normal life and development of teenage sons and daughters. Because teenage years are so volatile, signs of drug abuse can be misleading or hard to read. Parents who don't know their children very well and who don't pay attention to them will, of course, get the biggest surprises. They are most likely to deny problems or to become alarmed at the first sniff of pot or alcohol.

Nonetheless, there are danger signs to watch for:

- Unexplained absences from school, particularly on Monday morning and Friday afternoon
- Erratic school performance
- Extreme, unpredictable mood swings
- Smell of alcohol on breath; smell of pot in a teenager's bedroom
- Concern by classmates
- Drinking or pot smoking before exams
- Close friends who have drug-related problems

Checklists of danger signals are helpful as long as they do not replace attention, observation, and effective communication in confronting the issue of teenage drugs. Although the following checklist is focused on drinking, its relevance to all drug problems is self-evident. According to Alcoholics Anonymous, a yes to one question is a warning; a yes to as few as three questions points to a serious problem. How would your teenager answer these questions?

---

[11]Quoted in *New York Times,* July 19, 1981.

65

1. Do you lose time from school because of drinking?
2. Do you drink to overcome shyness and build up self-confidence?
3. Is drinking affecting your reputation?
4. Do you drink to escape from study or home worries?
5. Does it bother you if somebody says maybe you drink too much?
6. Do you have to take a drink to go out on a date?
7. Do you ever get into money trouble because of buying liquor?
8. Have you lost any friends since you started drinking?
9. Do you hang out with a crowd of heavy drinkers?
10. Do your old friends drink less than you do?
11. Do you drink until the bottle is empty?
12. Have you ever had a loss of memory from drinking?
13. Has drunk driving ever put you into a hospital or a jail?
14. Do you get annoyed with classes or lectures on drinking?
15. Do *you* think you have a problem with drinking?[12]

Distinguishing between use and abuse is particularly difficult because experimentation is a major part of growing up. Teen years are discovery years, which means trying and finding out. Teenagers are busily trying out different clothes, friends, hobbies, sports, music, movies, fads, fashions, opinions—even beliefs. They live in a world of incredible choices—a world that can be summed up by the advertising slogan, "Try it. You'll like it." They are imbued with the attitude that "you'll never know unless you try it." And so they try—beer, pot, and much more.

When drugs are not available, teenagers try incredible substitutes: drinking nutmeg or crushed aspirin in Coke, sniffing paint thinner or the vapors of burned plastic combs, consuming the cotton inserts from Vicks and Valo inhalers, smoking tea, injecting wine intravenously.[13] Fortunately, the use of inhalants and PCP, or "angel dust" (the

---

[12]Slightly adapted from the "Score-It-Yourself Quiz" from the pamphlet *Young People and A.A.* (New York: Alcoholics Anonymous World Services, Inc., 1969), p. 3.
[13]Examples cited by Harold J. Cornacchia, David E. Smith, and David J. Bentel in *Drugs in the Classroom,* 2nd ed. (St. Louis: C. V. Mosby Company, 1978), p. 46.

dangerous hallucinogen), declined in the late 1970s. But the use of amphetamines and other stimulants became more popular.[14]

When it comes to drugs, teenage experimentation is especially frightening for parents and teachers. They are not holding their breath as they do when a child learns to use a hammer. They are concerned with the question of whether their children or students are basically healthy or not. But what is healthy?

One health educator has commented that risk taking is part of being healthy—an observation that is cold comfort to anxious parents but reflects reality nonetheless. Robert D. Russell notes that healthy means "probably taking some risks, even a few major ones now and again." He calls it unhealthy "when the individual takes too many risks or loses too often." Noting that being healthy means functioning, he concludes: "Risk taking is necessary for healthy functioning. . . . The individual who takes a risk (with some caution perhaps) succeeds, then more confidently faces the next set of life choices."[15]

Instead of asking which kind of drug is worse—pot or alcohol—we suggest that parents face the significant question of whether teenagers are experimenting or evading, whether they are trying and occasionally indulging in drugs or are depending on them, whether drugs have become a short-term solution that creates serious problems.

Dr. Stephen F. Wepner of Fordham University's School of Education has extensive experience in school drug programs. He gets to the heart of the problem when he talks with teenagers: "I generally ask one question of those who say their involvement is limited to recreational use— parties, dances, and informal get-togethers. *Who is at the party—you or the drug?* Recognition of an inability to enjoy a social function without resorting to drugs is often enough of a motivation to get some youngsters thinking

---

[14]*New York Times,* February 19, 1981.
[15]Robert D. Russell, *Health Education* (Washington, D.C.: National Education Association, 1975), p. 115.

seriously about the implications of their behavior. It's a first step. Unfortunately, many then go home to watch their parents and their parents' friends drink themselves into oblivion at an *adult* gathering."[16]

Why Teenagers Turn to Drugs

When teenagers talk about drugs (including alcohol), it is clear that the more trouble they have in coping with life, the more attractive drugs become. For example:

> The first time I smoked a reefer I was eleven. My mother had to take care of the two of us all by herself and she never let us forget it. So every day I just smoked the smoke and I got the munchies and I got real fat. People would say, "Oh, there's fat Tawanna." So I got into a lot of fights and I didn't have friends so I just smoked some more.

> When I was a sophomore I was failing. I started getting high every day. It was a way I could get out of problems and just forget about them.[17]

> Academically, this was the most important year for college. S.A.T.'s and achievements, and I had finals coming up. I know I probably didn't want to cope or deal with the situation. It's easier to get drunk and not worry about it. Then again, you wake up the next morning and it's still there.[18]

> The kids who drank seemed to have something I wanted. I didn't know what it was. All I know is that I never felt I belonged anywhere. I felt close to them. Our common bond was self-pity.[19]

[16]Personal interview with one of the authors (Edward Wakin).
[17]Both quoted in *New York Times,* July 19, 1981.
[18]Norman and Harris, *Private Life,* pp. 87-88.
[19]*Newsweek,* January 8, 1979, p. 43.

I like getting high. When I first started, around thirteen or fourteen, I did it with my friends. Once in a while now I'll do it by myself. It relaxes you a lot. If you have a lot of problems, you forget them. Not really forget them, just put them aside for a little while. I use it as an escape.[20]

The reasons given by teenagers for turning to drugs break down into the following:

Peer-group pressure. Trying alcohol and marijuana has almost become a puberty rite. Friends and others their age make teenagers feel that it is part of the passage from child to teenager. Typically, when friends get together, saying no to a smoke or a drink means feeling left out. The offer is not a dare but an invitation to be part of the "in" group. Of course, parents cannot completely sanitize teenage contacts and experiences, but they can watch out for friends who may be a source of constant pressure for such conformity.

Curiosity. Drugs are part of the music scene—in the songs, among the performers, in the lingo. Drinking usually is as much a part of the adult family scene as dishes on the table. Teenagers invariably wonder what it is like to try drugs and what it feels like to get "high," particularly when the reports are often glowing and when they see their own parents and relatives tipsy.

Insecurity. In the transition time of adolescence, young people desperately want love and affection, recognition and comradeship. The less that need is met at home and in the family, the more apt teenagers are to fill that need by associating with other youngsters who drink and smoke together. Such associations are a shortcut to acceptance— no questions asked, no demands made. As one fourteen-year-old said of her high school in a comfortable middle-class area: "There are two groups in my school, the jocks and the burn-outs. The burn-outs smoke and take pills and

_____

[20]Norman and Harris, *Private Life*, p. 97.

69

drink, and the jocks are really into sports. You either take one way or another. If you're in the middle, you're nobody. If you're not good at sports, you don't have that much of a choice."[21]

Escape. Drugs, of all kinds, make it easier to run away from problems. Adults take drugs and thereby set the example for their children. The view of experts is that most teenagers develop the drinking practices of their parents: "The value placed on alcohol use, like other values, is first learned in the home. So, if a parent drinks heavily, regularly, for pleasure, to escape, socially, or not at all, usually the adolescent will initially drink the same way. . . . Peers form a secondary influence."[22] Since teenagers do not make the same distinctions among drugs that adults do, they may turn to pot rather than to alcohol. In either case, they may be applying a lesson learned by watching their parents.

Rebelliousness. Once a dominant motif in the drug scene, youthful rebellion has subsided as a widespread social phenomenon, but individual rebellion is still part of being a teenager. When teachers, parents, and other authority figures are seen as oppressors, drugs are a handy tool for acting out against them. Sometimes, drugs provide one of the few ways by which teenagers get their parents to pay attention to them.

Risk taking. This is basic to the teenage need to experiment, to try drugs, to see how many beers they can handle, to see what happens after a few joints. Since teenagers typically feel indestructible, they take risks that would appall their parents. Drugs solve the problem of what to do when teenagers get together and risk taking rises to the top of the agenda. It is a handy antidote to the teenage complaint about boredom. In the view of health educator

[21]*New York Times,* July 19, 1981.
[22]Peter Finn and Patricia A. O'Gorman, *Teaching about Alcohol* (Boston: Allyn & Bacon, n.d.), p. 33.

Harold J. Cornacchia and his colleagues, risk-taking behavior is "probably most important, both for the experimenting young and for those who become dependent."[23]

Sorting Things Out

In this context, it is shortsighted to fly off the handle at the first scent of pot or alcohol. Parents need to sort out three major ingredients as they face the question of *use* (from trying to occasionally getting high) or *abuse*. This is tricky territory. Some parents may misinterpret this discussion as approval of drug use and ignore our starting point: the reality that drugs, including alcohol, are widespread. Others may want an ironclad measuring standard to determine when occasional use becomes abuse. There is no escaping the realistic answer that *it all depends*. To that end, we suggest confronting the following in terms of each teenager, who is unique in his or her own right.

1. The environment
2. The process of growing up
3. The individual teenager

The environment. Since the teenager's environment begins at home, the basic lesson about drugs is learned there—not from preachments but from the attitudes and the behavior of parents. Parents are understandably weary of hearing such advice, but there is no getting around it. Sons and daughters take everything in, particularly whatever mother and father are convinced they are hiding. Consider the simple remark, "Boy, do I need a drink after the day I've had." Take it from there.

The other teenage environment is school, which elicits reactions that range from "I look forward to it" to "I hate it." Most schools and most students probably are located between those extremes, but enough is wrong with schools to bring about alienation and unrest. One educator

---

[23]Cornacchia, Smith, and Bentel, *Drugs in the Classroom*, p. 52.

has been scathing in describing "present conventional schools" as the "most inhumane institutions in America. . . . They closely rival the prisons; the only difference is that after 3 P.M. and on weekends we let the prisoners escape."[24]

Harsh? Yes.

Exaggerated? Certainly from the viewpoint of most teachers. But enough of that feeling exists among students to foster alienation and unrest, which, in turn, foster drug taking among students.

So we suggest asking these questions about school: Is the teenager alienated from his or her school? How much of the blame rests with the school? How important is the drug scene at the school? The answers will influence what happens with teenagers at school.

But teenagers are not the only ones with drug problems. The entire country has a problem with alcohol and other drugs. There are 10 million alcoholics in the United States, and many more millions are affected by the disease of alcoholism, which is the country's third most serious threat to health (after cancer and heart disease). One survey reported that one out of four women over thirty have prescriptions for amphetamines, barbiturates, or tranquilizers. Among higher income families, the proportion rises to almost one-half. As one trio of experts noted, "drug use of some sort has become a *social norm* in our drug-oriented culture."[25]

The mass media, which saturate the lives of young Americans, add their contribution to the drug culture. Television, in particular, is an escapist medium par excellence, followed closely by the youth-oriented movies that draw millions of teenagers. Even the terms of TV viewing and drugs have become interchangeable: *tuning in, tuning out, turning on, turning off*. Drugs fit easily into a media

---

[24]D. E. Glines, *Creating Humane Schools* (Mankato, Minn.: Campus Publishers, 1971).

[25]The survey of women and the comment are from Cornacchia, Smith, and Bentel, *Drugs in the Classroom*, p. 46.

environment that fosters escapism and preaches easy solutions (whether in TV dramatic shows or the commercials after every break).

The moral of the environment is unavoidable: It is a family fight against the general atmosphere of drug permissiveness—a fight that becomes harder if and when school also becomes part of the problem.

The process of growing up. A second look at teenage reasons for using drugs reveals that each reason is part of adolescence. In growing up, teenagers face peer-group pressure, are curious and insecure, are tempted to escape from their problems, feel rebellious and bored, like to take risks. Drugs are an outlet as well as an opportunity for these teenage needs and tendencies. But they are only one—and the wrong one at that.

Fortunately, teenagers usually choose more constructive or at least harmless alternatives. The list of alternatives is long and ranges from athletics and hobbies to dancing and extracurricular activities, from music and dramatics to political action. The more active and involved a teenager is, the less likely he or she is to become involved in drug abuse. There is neither the need nor the time. There is no vacuum to fill.

The individual teenager. Since no universal timetable applies to the teen years, adolescence is a unique experience. Teenagers develop and confront the many facets of growing up at different times and under various circumstances. The goal is responsible decision making by young people themselves, helped and supported by parents and teachers. At some unpredictable point, the young person becomes able to make decisions on his or her own. This ability involves becoming a mature adult, which is as elusive a category as its stereotyped opposite—irresponsible teenager.

IN A NUTSHELL

Because alcohol and other drugs are so widespread, parents must face the uncomfortable reality that they can not insulate their sons and daughters from exposure and experimentation. The statistics, the studies, and the surveys show that the great majority of teenagers are trying drugs of one kind or another (alcohol included). But teenagers don't need social scientists to tell them what is part of their daily lives. For their part, teenagers turn to drugs for various reasons: peer-group pressure, curiosity, insecurity, escape, rebelliousness, risk taking.

Teenagers are surrounded by a drug culture, ranging from what goes on in or around schools to the quick-fix messages of TV commercials. They face the pressures of growing up and the temptation to take drugs as a way to cope with the problems and anxieties of adolescence. Irresponsible decisions on drugs can have life-shattering consequences. The goal for each teenager—individual, unique, distinctive—is to make responsible decisions.

DISCUSSION EXTENDERS

1. Do you agree that alcohol is a drug? How is it viewed in your home?

2. Has your son or daughter ever seen you drink to excess? Ever seen excessive drinking in your home? Was it ever discussed afterward?

3. Should your son or daughter "learn to drink" at home?

4. What is in your medicine cabinet? How would you describe its contents in terms of drugs?

5. Have you ever discussed drugs with your children? How do you view the issue of pot versus alcohol?

6. What do the teachers and principal say about the drug scene at school?

7. What is your view of teenage experimentation with drugs? Would your son or daughter tell you the truth if you asked whether he or she had experimented? Should you ask?

8. Have you ever asked parents of a child with drug problems how they discovered the problem? What were the signs pointing in that direction?

9. What signs indicate that your teenager is having a "tough time"? How do you distinguish between passing problems and chronic ones? What signs of trouble do you watch for in your teenage son or daughter?

10. Has your son or daughter ever exhibited any of the danger signals in the checklist on page 66? How would you handle the situation if your teenager answered yes to one or more of the questions?

CHAPTER 5

Parents, Teenagers, and Sex

Ask teenagers what they would tell their parents about the teen sex scene and you will get plenty to talk about and even more to think about. In preparation for giving a talk to parents, one of us asked his high school students what they would tell their parents. The following sample responses were written by boys in their junior year.

First, they asked for better communication between the generations.

> I believe most parents today are scared witless about discussing sex. Their attitudes are very puritanical and archaic. Sex is a vital function in one's life. Teenagers should receive the proper training on sex. This should come from home. Nobody knows the teenagers better than their parents. I think they'll respect them more for that. Believe me, I never had that "talk." I learned it from the streets. Thank God I'm intelligent, because I was able to straighten myself out.

> Tell them not to worry. During all these years of our childhood, they have taught us the good and the bad. Now it's our turn to put those

teachings into practice. Although it's a rough world and we make hasty decisions sometimes, what we really need is open relationships. We don't want to come to them to get scolded, we want to talk and have them listen to us.

No one would quarrel with these sentiments. Unfortunately, many parents have trouble talking with their children, especially about sex. Not all parents who experience this block are "puritanical and archaic." Sometimes, to be sure, there are vestiges of false guilt and repression, but often the problem is simply a lack of communication skills, complicated by well-founded fears that their children may be sexually active before they can handle the consequences. Attitudes like those expressed in the following samples are tough to handle.

I think it's important for parents to know when their children are *really* in love and when they are just infatuated. . . . I'm pretty sure if the parents were really sure that the kids were as in love as they say they were, they'd be more accepting of their kids having sex. If you're really in love, there is nothing wrong with sex.

Tell the parents that their children love them very much and that they appreciate their concern for their safety. Most teenagers agree that haphazard premarital sex is wrong, but in cases where there is an intimate relationship, sex is a beautiful thing and can be engaged in, even though there may be consequences.

When the "consequences" can be venereal disease or pregnancy, there is not much consolation in knowing that it was a "beautiful thing." Nor is the fear of these consequences unreasonable. Venereal disease among teenagers becomes more prevalent every year. The number of out-of-wedlock births to teenagers rose dramatically throughout the 1970s—from one-third to almost one-half of the births to teenage girls between 1971 and 1979. Well over a million unmarried teenage girls get pregnant every year. In such a context, the following teen message is particularly challenging.

> Many people have negative attitudes toward sex. This only creates problems. Teenagers are always rebelling against authority; and if authority says "No Sex!" they will have it to spite authority. Parents should teach and explain sex to their children, not just the mechanics but also the consequences, and their own opinions and feelings. Parents shouldn't force their values on their children. They should be open and receptive to their children's sexual problems.

Parents *have* to respond, and that means much more than just putting their foot down. Like it or not, in families today, pronouncements from on high are like raindrops on a tin roof. Teenagers want a dialogue, not a dictum.

> If you're against premarital sex, don't impose an edict on your teenager. This only leads to rebellion and rejection of your ideas. Instead, sit down and explain your views adult to adult, and if your reasoning is sound, you will accomplish the most you could hope for and the best. [This comment is from a teenager who is against premarital sex.]

> By continually emphasizing that premarital sex is wrong it often makes the kids curious. Most of the time the parents don't even give reasons why we shouldn't have premarital sex; I know my parents didn't. They didn't really say anything at all.

But what do you say? And how do you say it? How can you get a hearing when it's the youngster who doesn't want to listen? Suppose it's *your* kid who wrote:

> Old people never want kids to do anything.
> They should mind their own business.

That's discouraging, all right. But many young people are much more open, much more sensible:

> If two kids want to have sex there is very little a parent can do to stop them. They will find a way. Parents should try to foresee the situation beforehand and have an honest discussion with the teenager. They should make very clear the consequences of premarital sex. Most importantly, they should erase the myths surrounding sex and make sure the teenager is well informed. A parent should be compassionate towards the problem of the teenager and warn him or her of the emotional impact and repercussions of teenage sex. Finally they should be loving and understanding, not vindictive and close-minded.

Myths about Sex

The myths to which this perceptive young man refers are many and persistent, particularly a favorite shibboleth of the 1980s: "Love makes it right." In a sense, the statement is valid. Real loves includes commitment, and marriage is the public, irrevocable declaration of that commitment. But for teenagers—and for depressingly large numbers of adults—love and commitment are miles apart.

Adolescents are understandably prone to confuse infatuation with love. Teenage relationships can be very beautiful and meaningful and can foster real personal growth, but they are not likely to last. It is unwise to make too great an emotional investment in such relationships, and they certainly do not justify the kind of intimacy that is appropriate for married people. With help, most youngsters can see this and accept it without feeling put down:

> Teenage love is an infatuation. I say this because teenagers are experiencing deep emotional, social,

and physiological stress during these years. What is love to them one day can be a result of a massive hormone influx, when viewed with hindsight. Teenagers still have a long way to go in developing their emotional and mental attitudes, before they are ready for real love.

Still, a wistful note is struck by this teenager:

> I think that parents of today have no concept of how *truly* close two young people can be. Without having sex enter the discussion, parents just don't think it's possible for a guy and a girl to be deeply committed to each other.

Closely allied to the myth that "love makes it right" is this old chestnut: "If you love each other, you don't need a piece of paper to make it right." The piece of paper, of course, is the marriage license. The shallowness of this slogan may seem too obvious to need refutation, but many intelligent and even mature adolescents need help to understand the fallacy.

The taboo on premarital intercourse rests ultimately on very solid ground, but many adults who know it instinctively are hard pressed to explain why. We are likely to repeat the traditional warnings against pregnancy and venereal disease. These are still good arguments, well borne out by alarming statistics, but they have been undercut by medical progress, especially in the development of birth control methods. So we must face the question, rarely articulated by adolescents but felt by them: Suppose you're lucky, or careful, or both, and avoid VD and pregnancy. Are these the only possible harmful consequences of acting on the principle that "love makes it right"?

To answer this question, we must view it in terms of what we want for our children—not in terms of what we are afraid will happen to them. Basically, teenagers want what parents want for them in fulfilling the best possibilities of their sexuality—to become generous, affectionate, caring people, capable of loving and being loved. Parents want teenagers to learn how to form and nurture meaningful heterosexual relationships characterized by honesty, integrity, responsiveness, and sensitivity. Both know that those are the qualities that make a marriage work—qualities that make good wives and husbands, good mothers and fathers. Teenagers know that, and somewhere down the road most of them are destined to "settle down" and marry and have families. They also know that many marriages do not last, that commitments are hard to live up to. More and more of them have direct experience of this as children in one-parent families.

So how are teenagers supposed to develop this arsenal of virtues? How does one learn to be a lover and to integrate sexuality into one's whole life project? This is what teenagers want desperately to know, and many have no one to tell them. But before trying to tell them, let's look at what the competition has to say.

Outside Pressures

Who is the competition? An imposing array of manipulators and exploiters and misguided do-gooders. These include songwriters, movie and television scriptwriters, the barons of the multibillion-dollar sex industry, Planned Parenthood, and just plain other kids. Let's consider each of these formidable adversaries in turn, so that parents can take into account what and whom they are up against.

The writers of the Top Forty Tunes in any given week have lyrical messages to go with the big beat that assaults the ears and psyches of their young fans. The messages are crudely sexual: sex is fun; sex is great; don't wait, get it while you can; sex is no problem unless you make it one; and if you aren't getting it or aren't looking for it, there's something wrong with you. When the message is not a hard sell of recreational sex, a simplistic hymn to relational sex has an unspoken premise: intimacy demands no commitment or responsibility, only the "honest" feeling of the moment that looks no further and makes no demands.

Scriptwriters who grind out soaps and sitcoms generally have pretty much the same message. They take it for granted that everyone has a right to sexual intimacy simply by wanting it, and that those who would say otherwise are hung-up puritans or dreamers. The people who run the booming sex industry are a shadowy group, harder to identify; but it is clear that they profit from all this propaganda. Sex is not just available; it is thrust upon the young long before they are old enough to know they are being manipulated.

The Planned Parenthood people mean well, but their attempts to help are at best inadequate and at worst a disaster. They begin by sharing a common concern about the epidemic of teenage pregnancy and abortion. Their solution is pragmatic and as American as apple pie: teach about contraceptives, make them available, and motivate boys and girls to use them. They consider it inevitable that the young are going to have sex, so they try to teach them how to have sex without consequences.

Even within this narrow, self-imposed perspective, the Planned Parenthood strategy does not work. Most of the youngsters, especially the girls, are psychologically unable to "plan ahead"; for them, the experience must have at least the appearance of spontaneity. In one survey, six out of ten sexually active teenagers reported that they do not use birth-control methods or use them only some of the time.[1] Another survey of young people in metropolitan areas indicates that there has indeed been an increase in the use of contraceptives but also an increase in the number of unwanted pregnancies. No one should be surprised by these findings. The weakness in the Planned Parenthood strategy was pointed out some years ago by Archbishop Joseph Bernardin:

> What is the alternative [to promoting contraceptives]? I believe there is one, but I do not think it is easy. . . . It amounts to turning things around and, instead of telling teenagers that they can have sex without consequences, telling them

---

[1] Jane Norman and Myron W. Harris, *The Private Life of the American Teenager* (New York: Rawson, Wade Publishers, 1981), p. 42.

the truth: There is no such thing as sex without consequences, whether these be emotional, physical, social—or all three.

It amounts, in other words, to telling them what they need to know anyway. Sex is not merely for fun or for the expression of transitory affection. It is an enriching and serious business between mature people who are emotionally, socially, and even economically able to accept the consequences, of which pregnancy is hardly the only one.

I agree that more education of teenagers . . . is needed. But I believe it should be education in such things as family values, a healthy and integrated acceptance of sexuality, stability in marital relationships, a sense of obligation toward other persons, and willingness to accept the consequences of one's actions. In other words, it should seek to help them grow up as sexually mature adults.[2]

Finally, teenagers face the tyranny of their peers and feel pulled in different directions, as shown in this testimony by a young man in the third year of high school:

In our society there is a lot of pressure put on teenagers. Much of it deals with how they should handle sex. Our society in itself is constantly changing; no longer are there any set norms to be followed.

As an adolescent grows older, he tries to act independently of his parents. During this time, he looks to the peer group for acceptance and guidance. Peer pressure at this time is tremendous. You want to be accepted as sexually normal. The easiest way to accomplish this is to act as the rest of your friends do. If your friends have a

---

[2]Quoted in *New York Times,* January 22, 1978.

more exciting social life than you do, you stick out. Some people will accuse you of homosexuality only to increase their own status. These accusations can have a horrible effect on your life. Rumors do not stop easily; they can destroy someone.

When you date a girl, the peer group tells you to push, go as far as you can. They expect a good story. In their eyes, the girl is a toy you use for fun and status. They don't care about her as a person at all. Often the ideal is to "love them and leave them."

Your parents usually have a different view of how you should behave sexually. At times, it seems as if they can only see the negative side of your sexual encounters. Do they forget kissing and petting are enjoyable? It is natural for people to be curious about something society treats as magically as sex. Now here you are: the peer group says push her, and your parents say wait.

Girls are going through much the same situation. Society seems to condone premarital sex and attack unwed mothers. . . . Both you and your girlfriend are under pressure. I don't feel it is right for you to pressure each other even more. . . .

People are not toys; you cannot play with them and put them away. It takes courage to stand up against peer pressure, but I think we should try. Your friends are as confused as you are.

Countering Outside Pressures

To help teenagers cope with these pressures, it is tempting to become argumentative and strident and to make bad arguments for good causes. To counter those who trivialize sex, it is tempting to place sex on such an exalted pedestal that the pleasure seems drained out of it. To counter promiscuity, it is tempting to be so adamant that the teenager sees only a puritanical, up-tight parent.

The outside pressures are powerful enough without parents undermining themselves.

The first task is to assess our own feelings about our own and others' sexuality. God "made us male and female; in His own image He created us" (Genesis 1:27). To have a positive, outgoing attitude toward our own maleness or femaleness and to be comfortable with our own bodies and accepting of ourselves, we must be able to express affection and love with our whole person. This is not as easy as it sounds, particularly for those of us who grew up in an atmosphere that denied and repressed sensuality.

It is not enough for us to be against bad sex; we have to be for good sex. If our children perceive us as incapable of positive, joyful sex, they will not look to us for guidance. Indeed, why should they? What could we offer them besides threats, warnings, and prophecies of doom? When teenagers ask for communication, they are looking for more than logical, well-thought-out arguments against premarital sex. They are looking for feelings and attitudes with which they can identify and be comfortable.

Teenagers also need to see and experience, in their own families, the free and easy expression of affection. They need to be listened to, to feel accepted, to feel warmth. They need to be hugged. These powerful, nonverbal forms of communication enable them to realize that sex is more than genitality, that it embraces many levels of intimacy, of which intercourse is but one.

Children first learn about sex through such nonverbal communication. Life in the family "talks" to them incessantly about human relationships. When family members are unabashed in their physical and verbal expression of love and affection, children are powerfully influenced for good. When children grow up not only being, but also *perceiving* themselves as, unconditionally loved by those closest to them, they develop a sense of self-worth and personal significance. These experiences are a powerful antidote against inducements to sexual exploitation, which offers a counterfeit version of love to those who feel most deprived of it. The young people who are hardest to fool are those who know they already have the real thing.

86

From all that has preceded, it is obvious that sex education is a must for young people in spite of those parents who see formal sex instruction as just one more assault on their children's innocence. They fear that such instruction may give youngsters ideas that would not otherwise occur to them. They are hoping the whole problem will go away if educators just stop talking about it.

But wishing will not make it so, neither in sex nor in drugs. Sex is everywhere in our society—no less so in the world of teenagers. Even without outside pressures, it is biologically impossible for teenagers not to think about sex. In a self-portrait drawn by teenagers in the late 1970s, the obvious was confirmed: 68 percent said they "often think about sex." Almost eight out of ten (78 percent) felt that "dirty jokes are fun at times" (compared with 58 percent in the 1960s).[3] There are even more startling findings in the Norman-Harris survey of teenagers:

- Nearly one out of three thirteen- to fifteen-year-olds said they have had sexual intercourse.
- Nearly six out of ten sixteen- to eighteen-year-olds said they have had sexual intercourse.[4]

Faced with the realities of American life, the conclusion of a *New York Times* editorialist seems inescapable: it is "cruel" to leave teenagers unarmed and without responsible sex education in the face of the sexual revolution. Teenagers want to know; and if they do not learn about sex in a responsible way from a responsible source, they will go elsewhere. We recommend the argument in the *Times* editorial that opponents of sex education want "another world":

> Regret over the sweep of the American sexual revolution is understandable, but reluctance to deal with its consequences is cruel. Today's

---

[3] Daniel Offer, Eric Ostrov, Kenneth I. Howard, *The Adolescent: A Psychological Self-Portrait* (New York: Basic Books, 1981), Table E-7.
[4] Norman and Harris, *Private Life*, p. 42.

teenagers didn't make that revolution, they were born into it. And for adults to deny them the information to which they as human beings are entitled is to make them its victims.[5]

When to Discuss Sex

When is the right time to talk to children about sex? Obviously, there is no hard-and-fast rule for every child, even within the same family, but *better too soon than too late.* And "too late" is coming sooner and sooner. Children are growing up faster than ever, both physically and in terms of sexual awareness. Parents who were teenagers in the 1950s grew up in a time that called for drastically different timetables and tactics. While human nature does not change, cultural patterns do and they make a very big difference. The basic guideline is that boys and girls should be told about puberty before it happens to them.

If we get off on the right foot, there is a good chance that the lines of communication will remain open throughout the adolescent years. Ten- and twelve-year-olds need and can handle a limited amount of information. Later on, in high school years, they need help in understanding and dealing with more complex matters, such as new and powerful emotions, relationships, and intimacy. The following straight talk from a sex educator describes the teenage situation.

> With the onset of menstruation and breast development in girls, of seminal emission and more frequent erection in boys, and the growth of pubic hair in both, new attention to and worry about self are added to the burdens of the young person. Accompanying these physical changes are fantasies and feelings never dealt with before, not to mention moodiness and unusual desires. Underlying it all are the troublesome questions:

[5]*New York Times,* as quoted in Joel Wells, *How to Survive with Your Teenager* (Chicago: Thomas More Press, 1982), p. 61.

Am I okay? How do I compare with others? The turmoil of this inner world can drive the youngster to hasty action or into the doldrums of depression. At a time when the need for understanding and help is so urgent, the young person becomes distant and unable to express himself or herself.[6]

These concerns are so personal that the adolescent may be reluctant to share them with any adult, even with a parent who communicates very well. As sensitive parents, we know and accept this. We do not want to pry into our growing children's lives. What is important is that they know we both respect their privacy and care about them and that we are always there when they need us.

Sometimes it is easier for youngsters to accept help from teachers and counselors in school. These people can often give the kind of assistance that either parents are unable to offer their children or children are unable to seek or accept from their parents. That is why parents should check out their children's elementary and secondary schools to see what kind of programs are being provided.

Some sex-education programs are effective; others are not. Some may have features that conflict with parental religious or moral values. There may be no program at all. Try to approach this subject, either as an individual parent or through the PTA, in a positive manner. Be open to new ideas and perspectives; presume the goodwill of all involved. But ask questions and be critical in your evaluation of what is or is not being done. This is a subject where good people can and do differ and where even the best and the wisest feel threatened, making it difficult to disagree calmly and constructively. The issue is easily sidetracked to a battle over the sexual revolution instead of the best means for helping young people develop a healthy and responsible sexuality.

---

[6]Gordon Lester, *When It's Time to Talk about Sex* (St. Meinrad, Ind.: Abbey Press, 1981), p. 60.

Sex Roles

Starting at home, boys and girls learn to treat members of the opposite sex with respect, beginning with the example of their parents. Sexual stereotyping of boys as "macho" and of girls as second-class runs counter to the development of healthy, sharing relationships. Even the most enlightened parents need to fight against tendencies to assume that their sons and daughters must fit preconceived notions.

Fathers still tend to view sons as athletic rather than artistic. Teenage boys with aesthetic interests may get hassled by their friends and thus need affirmation, not more pressure, from their fathers. Teenage boys are also sensitive to charges, overt or implied, of homosexuality; they want desperately to be "normal." In some circles, the mere failure to be a jock is grounds for ostracism. Parents cannot eliminate this kind of pressure, but they can refrain from adding to it. The pressure starts when children are very young—when little boys learn that their sisters may cry but they may not, that girls are made of sugar and spice and everything nice but boys are supposed to be rough and tumble and are not allowed to show their feelings, that the man is always in charge, and so on.

Girls also need reinforcement at home as women's self-image and expectations change for the better and as women break out of rigidly conventional roles. One does not have to be an uncritical fan of the women's movement to rejoice in the hard-earned victories against male chauvinism. But little girls are still made to feel, ever so subtly, that they belong to the *second* sex, that certain ambitions are appropriate for their brothers but not for them, that being assertive or aggressive or even smart is somehow less feminine, that the woman's job is to please the man who must always feel like the boss, and so on. When a girl becomes a teenager, she needs the awareness that she enjoys first-class citizenship and that she does not have to underplay her part to avoid threatening a boy. Whether she gets married or not, she can then see herself as a person with equal rights and dignity, not a role player whose lines have already been written.

Speaking of Pornography

Teenage excursions into pornography traumatize some parents while others take this in stride, but sooner or later the issue comes up. We advise strongly against over-reacting. Shock, surprise, horror, and indignation tend to undermine a parent's credibility. Teenagers then feel that the parent is either denying what is going on (and therefore is not "with it") or is double-talking (has the parent never seen an R-rated movie?). For their part, teenagers want to pursue their curiosity. (For those cut off from responsible sex information and guidance at home and at school, that curiosity is strongest.)

There are a number of things that parents can do to discourage their teenagers from seeking pornography. They can let them know, quietly and firmly, that they do not approve of pornography. They can tell them that they understand the fascination and attraction of pornography. They can try to get across, at a level their youngsters can comprehend, the reasons why pornography is bad: not because it is "dirty" (our sexuality comes from God and is something good) but because it makes it hard for people to appreciate one another. It makes people into things and uses and abuses them.

There is a paradox here. Teenagers turn to pornography because they want to see *everything*. But that's just what's wrong with porn: it doesn't show everything! Far from revealing too much, it reveals too little. In its obsession with the body, pornography conceals the richness of the whole person. Here is the real evil of pornography. Sexuality is meant to get us out of ourselves and to open us up to other people in love. Pornography debases the other and turns us in on ourselves; it inhibits growth. Young people can understand messages like these, provided they are delivered without contradictory emotional overtones. Then they can begin to see that pornography is not something for grown-ups, but rather something to be outgrown.

Teenagers who have healthy attitudes toward sex and a good image of themselves are not very promising customers for porn, hard or soft. The adult magazines and peep shows will always be around, and the civil authorities do what they can on the public level to stem the tide. Parents can administer an effective antidote at home by giving their children positive experiences and attitudes. Pornography becomes a serious problem for the individual when it moves into a vacuum of ignorance, loneliness, or self-rejection. Providing good information, friendship, and affirmation fills that vacuum.

Touchy Issues

Masturbation, once a highly sensitive issue for the majority of parents, is a matter of decreasing concern. The focus has changed from viewing it as a moral problem to viewing it as a problem of growth. It is a common experience among adolescents, especially males, and becomes a problem only when it becomes a habit. Then, it could be a symptom of some psychological disorder that requires counseling.

Experience indicates that focusing on masturbation itself nearly always aggravates the problem. It creates anxiety, increases preoccupation, and by a kind of vicious circle ends up exacerbating the very problem it tries to solve. As in the case of pornography, both the problem and the solution lie elsewhere—in the need for affection, friendship, and self-esteem.

Another source of anxiety is fear of homosexuality. Although attitudes are changing here, mostly for the better, there is still an enormous amount of social pressure on those who are gay or considered to be so. Some youngsters suffer from an unfounded fear that they may be homosexual, either because they have not lived up to exaggerated cultural expectations about how a "real" man or woman is supposed to feel or act, or because they have had isolated experiences of sexual exploration with members of the same sex. A few words of encouragement or enlightenment from well-informed adults can dispel these fears and assure them that they are quite "normal."

But suppose a child *is* homosexual. This is hard to accept, and many a family has been torn apart by guilt and rejection when parents realize (or, worse, refuse to acknowledge) that a child is homosexual. There is no use in pretending that this is of no great importance. No matter how enlightened or tolerant society may become, acknowledging homosexuality is always going to be a source of suffering for the homosexual and for his or her family. The first thing that must be said—and we cannot say it strongly enough—is that no parent should feel guilty. It was once believed that homosexuality was a condition caused by certain relational patterns within the family. That theory is bankrupt, and now the only thing that can be said with certainty about the causes of homosexuality is that they simply are not known. The important thing is to cope with reality as best we can.

What is that reality? The American Psychological Association has gone on record that whatever homosexuality is, it is not a sickness. The highest teaching authority of the Catholic church attaches no moral stigma to *being* homosexual, only to acting out homosexuality through physical expression; and on the latter point, significant numbers of Protestant and Catholic moralists disagree.[7]

Only rarely can homosexual tendencies be reversed. When it becomes clear that such tendencies cannot be reversed, then the only sensible prescription calls for large doses of love and acceptance. The rights of homosexuals are being increasingly recognized, and this recognition should start in the home. Despite the sometimes strident rhetoric of gay liberationists, homosexuality is not simply a different preference, just as acceptable as heterosexuality. It is a very real liability. But there are many handicaps that people overcome, and this can be one of them.[8]

Facing Crises

Even in the best families, kids do get in trouble: they contact venereal disease and they get pregnant. If parents

---

[7]Catholic Theological Society of America, *Human Sexuality* (New York: Doubleday & Co., 1979), p. 228.
[8]Cf. R. Nugent, "Homosexuality and the Hurting Family," *America*, February 28, 1981.

take the attitude that "it could never happen to us," they may be asking for even more trouble. It is most important that teenagers be convinced that they can bring *any* problem to their parents and get support. They should not have to turn to confidential outside agencies.

Sure, it is heartbreaking to learn that your daughter is pregnant or that your son has gotten someone else's daughter pregnant. You want to make loud noises or throw something breakable or kick in the nearest wall. But that doesn't help, and it just makes it harder for your son or daughter who is already miserable or frightened. Make up your mind now that you will do everything to protect your children, but that once they are in trouble—no matter what it is—you will stick by them. If you are capable of this kind of hard-nosed loyalty, they will know it and they will come to you for help rather than to strangers.

This chapter is ending on a grim note after an intimidating view of the teen sex scene. Actually, most youngsters are going to navigate the waters of adolescent sexuality without any serious mishaps. But the problems are real, and we should try to face them as best we can, remembering what the teenager said at the beginning of this chapter: "Although it's a rough world and we make hasty decisions sometimes, what we really need is open relationships. We don't want to come to [our parents] to get scolded, we want to talk and have them listen to us."

It is not always easy to listen, and the temptation to scold is great. Resist it. As Mary Calderone has pointed out, the issue is not sex, but love—your love for your child.

> I think fear of sex is the greatest sex-related problem in this country. The fear of the unnameable, the unthinkable, the undoable—fear brings silence, and silence breeds alienation. . . .
>
> The primary role of the family is to teach its children how to give and receive love. And that love has to be absolutely unqualified. If you're a parent and you learn today that your child is no longer a virgin, that she is pregnant, or that he or she is homosexual . . . the child is still the same

child he or she was yesterday, and the way you felt about her or him yesterday you can also feel today. That's unqualified love and support. And that's what the family is for—to prepare children for the life they are going to lead, not you. You've made your choices, had your life—now it's their turn.[9]

IN A NUTSHELL

When adolescents do not have open, honest discussion of sex with parents or other helping adults, the vacuum is filled by popular myths that encourage irresponsible behavior and experimentation. Parents who try to inculcate wholesome attitudes face opposition from many quarters. Mass media, peers, and the sex industry exploit young people's fears of inadequacy or ostracism by pressuring them into premature intimacy. Some social agencies reduce sex education to stategies for preventing venereal disease and pregnancy.

In countering these influences, parents and other adults must be not only against bad sex but for good sex. Puritanism, rigidity, false guilt, and repression undermine attempts at responsible sex education. Conversely, verbal and physical expressions of affection, especially in the home, reinforce healthy attitudes.

Explicit sex education is needed both at home and in school, not only in the form of information but in attitudes that counteract stereotypes. Problems such as pornography,

---

[9]"Why Parents Can't Say Enough About Sex," *U.S. Catholic,* October 1982, p. 32.

masturbation, and apparent homosexuality can and should be handled calmly and without overreacting. More serious problems like extramarital pregnancy and genuine homosexual orientation should elicit loyalty and support rather than rejection or condemnation. In all these crises, openness and love can succeed where silence and condemnation fail.

DISCUSSION EXTENDERS

1. What, in your opinion, inhibits free and open discussion of sex between parent and child? What helps?

2. Do you have any direct experience or factual information about the sex education programs in your children's schools? How do you evaluate these programs?

3. Do you agree that "there is no such thing as sex without consequences"? Do your experiences and observations support or contradict this view?

4. Do you find it as easy to be *for* good sex as it is to be *against* bad sex? How would you describe the differences between good and bad sex? How do you communicate to your children your attitudes about sex?

5. What do your teenagers think of the view of sex that is communicated by contemporary songs, movies, and TV programs? How do you deal with these influences?

6. What kind of nonverbal messages about sex do you think are communicated within your family?

7. Have your children ever confronted you with the problem of pornography? How did you handle it?

8. How do you try to bring up your girls as feminine and your boys as masculine? Do changing roles and expectations complicate this task for you?

9. Would you describe your ideas about homosexuals and homosexuality as tolerant and accepting? Do your feelings go along with your thinking?

10. What would you do if your unmarried teenage daughter became pregnant? If your unmarried teenage son got someone else's daughter pregnant?

CHAPTER 6

Believing Versus Belonging

If you listen long enough to teenagers describing their religious highs, you will notice two themes running through their accounts. One is an openness to contemplation: they speak of quiet walks along the seashore, times in the woods when they felt very close to nature. What adults might simply call meditative moods are perceived by teenagers as intensely religious.

The other theme is a hunger for friendship and community. Times of closeness—when masks fall away and intensely personal feelings are revealed in an atmosphere of honesty and trust—are seen as openings to the divine. The most popular and successful youth retreats are those that facilitate these joyful experiences of community. Such experiences are good news indeed to youngsters who often feel isolated, lonely, and locked within themselves.

Although teenagers have shown a receptivity—even hunger—for religious experience in recent years, much of this experience takes place outside the precincts of conventional religion. It happens, for example, in retreat settings or on Bible camp weekends, usually with other young people, under the guidance of those whose special ministry is to youth. At this time of their lives, when the world of childish religion is fading away and when they are still not at home in the world of adults, teenagers need to join with others their own age to express their strongest feelings. These privileged moments of religious awakening often carry a strong emotional content. Adults who downplay the expression of emotion in religion underestimate its importance among the young.

Organized religion faces a serious problem not so much in teen resistance to religion as in the organized, institutional setting of formal religion. This was reflected in a 1980 Gallup poll of teenagers:

> Although more than half of American teenagers believe religion can answer all or most of today's problems, as many as one teen in three feels religion is largely old-fashioned and out of date.
>
> However, although many teens feel that organized religion, in the institutional sense, is not relevant, most continue to believe in the basic ethical and moral precepts taught by the churches and synagogues in the United States.[1]

For many teenagers, this attitude leads to a subjectivistic individualism that, in effect, negates anything like religion in the formal sense. One eleventh grader epitomized such individualism:

> Religion limits you, makes you conform into a mold, and takes away your individuality. It's great for people who don't want the responsibility for their decisions. . . .
>
> I think the only religion people really need is their conscience. What they believe is right *is* right for them, as long as they truly believe it is right. I'm not saying this is good for everyone, but it's good for me.

For every youth like this one, there are several who still long for some larger, shared frame of meaning. They look

---

[1]*Emerging Trends*, Princeton (New Jersey) Religious Research Center, January 1981.

for God but are unable to find him in the forms of prayer they learned as children or in the gatherings of adults on Sunday. And so they drift, not because they are really irreligious, but because they are unable to find nourishment for the part of themselves that needs expression in religious symbols and actions.

Religion Teen-style

Glimpses into the religious world of the young yield helpful insights for adults who want to pass on their beliefs and traditions. For example, many adults set a high value on fidelity to routine. They express their religious convictions by saying prayers at set times, attending church every Sunday, and participating in the liturgy regularly. They tend to think of God as a lawgiver and judge who rewards people for fidelity and punishes them for neglecting their duties and obligations. The church is seen as the guardian of this arrangement, and the clergy are expected to reinforce these values of order and stability. This approach to Christianity, while containing much that is true and helpful, is rather incomplete. But no matter. The point is that this vision and this approach are quite foreign to the great majority of teenagers—not only the religiously lukewarm but even the fervently committed.

The way teenagers think about God, their approach to worship, and their expectations of church and clergy are markedly different. For teenagers, spontaneity is more important than routine; enthusiasm rates higher than regularity; warmth outranks propriety; and reverence is found more readily in shared community than in a sense of the sacred. Listen to this seventeen-year-old reacting to a Sunday sermon in which the congregants were called "Jesus' helpers":

> I disagree with this because I think of Jesus more as a partner and not a slave master. The church consistently preaches God as our master instead of friend. I disagree with this because you cannot have a close friendship between two

people if one of the two is constantly being placed on a pedestal. . . .

I am not condemning all churches, just those which refuse to change with the changing times and people. . . . The church must practice more peace and brotherhood if it wishes to survive.

Some will object to these comments as overstated or simplistic. Why can't God be our master as well as our friend? Why does Jesus' helper have to be a slave? But this misses the point. Adolescents and young adults often think in either/or categories. A God who could be both majestic and intimate, Lord as well as friend, may elude them. The kind of "God talk" that works with young people is discourse about a God who is friend, intimate, and lover, rather than a God who is Creator, Lord, and judge. Of course, God is all of these, and we should say so. But if certain aspects of God are more appealing than others for teenagers, we can with integrity place greater emphasis on these aspects in order to reach teenagers at their stage of development.

These ideas have important consequences for the way this new generation will express its faith. It is demanding a different religious style. Although many older people prefer a liturgy that is quiet, reverent, and reserved, the young look for warmth, interaction, relaxed spontaneity. If this sounds a bit like a comparison between organ and guitar, it is no coincidence. But teenage religious style goes far beyond a difference in musical expression; it represents a different way of thinking, feeling, and being together.

Teen Sense of Sin

The young also have a drastically different attitude toward sin. To say their sense of sin is sometimes tenuous and vague is an understatement. There is still some guilt around, but not nearly as much as there used to be; and it is much less clearly focused. When you stop thinking of God as lawgiver and judge, your ideas of sin, guilt, and forgiveness are inevitably going to be modified. For one thing, sin as the breaking of rules is going to yield to sin as a failure to love or as a rift in a relationship.

Consider the following "confession" of a high school student, written as a classroom exercise. He gave us permission to use it, though it is clearly personal.

> I have not done a really supermalicious deed. I didn't torch a building, murder someone or do anything serious. Instead, it is my neglect to show concern for others' feelings that is my main failing. . . .
>
> When my sister had volunteered me to help sell chances with her (so she wouldn't be alone), I got mad at her, told her I had no time for that. When she started to cry, I was only more caustic to her.
>
> I find myself growing more cynical toward my father every day. The other day at the dinner table, he told me *exactly* what happened at work that day. I had heard this story hundreds of times, so I just didn't listen. I looked out the window, asked someone to pass the ketchup, and then walked over and picked up the newspaper. I purposely disconcerned myself with my father because I know it would get him angry and "hurt" him.
>
> My friends at school are pretty nice kids, but many times I reply curtly, sarcastically or condescendingly. I don't know why I do it. I try to act like a big shot by being insulting and mean. Sometimes these comments get a few laughs, but I know that they actually hurt people. Maybe I'm cynical to get people to notice me. Sometimes I see the slight possibility of an abusive reply, so I don't say anything; I keep my feelings locked inside. That is how this sin of mine inhibits my evolution and growth as a human being.

This is an impressive example of religious self-awareness that is by no means unusual among young people. They have come a long way from yesteryear's laundry-list approach to the Ten Commandments. They have much more concern with personal growth and the quality of relationships.

In some ways, the teenage view of morality is an improvement over the old approach: less mechanical, less rigid; more concerned with human development than with reward and punishment. Surely, that's good news. On the other hand, it can sometimes be vague and lacking in substance. Some teenagers are poorly instructed in how to approach morality. About the only question they seem to ask themselves is, How do you feel about yourself? That's the bad news.

The mixed picture is a natural outcome of the changes that have taken place in recent years. Try to get away from a legalistic preoccupation with rules, and some people are bound to relax too much. Try to put away puritanical and repressive attitudes toward sex, and some are going to go too far. Try to go easy on the guilt, and some will conclude that anything goes. Tell people that God is not a stern taskmaster but a loving friend, and some will fashion for themselves a nice, grandfatherly deity who just wants whatever they want. Tell them that going to church should be not just the fulfillment of an obligation but a genuine religious experience, and some will drop out as soon as they feel that they are "not getting anything out of it." And so on. Young people today have been spared some of the hangups of their forebears, but they are sometimes poorer in other ways. Neither uncritical approval nor blanket condemnation is in order, but rather a discriminating recognition of both gains and losses in a new religious culture.

Religious Care and Treatment

Having drawn a general picture of how young people approach religion, we can now tackle specific questions that parents ask us: How can I help my children form a religious identity? Why don't churches teach religion the way they used to? How can I help my children grow up as believing and practicing members of my church? After diagnosis, here are our prescriptions for the religious care and treatment of the young.

First a reminder to parents: young people are greatly dependent for their religious development on the significant adults in their lives. So the first way to help your children is to do something not for them but for yourself. Check the depth and seriousness of your own religious commitment. Forget about the children for a minute and consider what your faith does for *you*. What resources for living does it give you that you could not get elsewhere? Outside of attending church on Sunday, what time or energy do you give to religious concerns and projects in an average week? When was the last time that you read a book or an article about your faith? How many serious conversations have you engaged in on religious matters in the last year? We are not trying to put you on the defensive in asking these questions. We are addressing a problem that besets Americans of all faiths—a tendency to think of religion as something mainly for children and to regard religious education and growth as happening only before adulthood.

Paradoxically, this child-centeredness is a serious obstacle to young people's religious growth. It implies that religion is something to be outgrown. When viewed in this way, faith becomes not a lifelong project but something that we finish early in life and then pass on to our children. Is it surprising, then, that adolescents tend to put away religion with the other accoutrements of childhood? Or that unchurched adults take nostalgia trips to church, especially at Christmas, to recapture their childhood?

On the other hand, if you are still working at religion and growing in your faith, you will help your youngsters. You will be teaching them by example. However, let us be very clear about the kind of example we mean. As today's children move into adolescence, they are no longer impressed by the fact that their parents spend an hour a week on religion. Whether or not they put it into words, they need tangible evidence that religion has a significant impact for good on people's lives. Conventional religion that has no discernible effect on values or life-style has a bad reputation among the young. Even where it is not explicitly rejected, it is not taken seriously.

How can parents give more convincing example? By investing time, talent, and energy in living out their faith. There are innumerable ways of doing this. Parents can join or assist church organizations such as the youth group, parish council, or home-school association. They can play an active part in religious services and church activities. They may participate in marriage-encounter weekends, retreats, or prayer meetings. They may serve on teams that help engaged couples prepare for marriage. They can read books about religion and subscribe to religious publications. These are just some concrete ways to give children tangible evidence of the conviction that religion is serious, grown-up business and an enriching part of life.

For teenagers, formation of a durable religious identity depends on more than uncritical adherence to customs and traditions. It must be perceived as bound up with conviction and choice. As this sixteen-year-old describes the religious journey in his life, think of what is happening to your own children.

As a young person looks at the world today, he sees problems everywhere but answers nowhere. It is very easy to see nothing of value in society or religion, and to withdraw into a state of indifference or hate. I have friends who find emptiness in life, and have the idea that the only possible purpose in life is to have fun and indulge yourself. . . . Many of these people find no meaning in life, and have "grown up" and can't believe in religion.

I had this attitude for some time, but quickly became dissatisfied with it and searched for something better. For some reason I still haven't figured out, I took a second look at that religion I used to believe in. Perhaps I was brainwashed with it in grammar school and church, but I still saw truth and meaning in Jesus' words. What he said made sense, for his time and today. I don't want to sound like a hyperactive evangelist, but I found meaning and purpose for life in Jesus and his message of love. For me, Jesus is the answer. I'm not saying that I accept and believe all the doctrines and teachings of the Catholic church, simply because I haven't really taken the time to analyze them all. In some areas, such as birth control, celibacy, and women in the priesthood, I am positively against the church's teaching. But yet I do accept much of the basic ideas of the church. . . . I have found my answer in Jesus. I honestly and truly believe in him as a friend who I can talk to and pray to for help and faith.

As intensely individual as this experience has been for this student, he acknowledges that it happened not in isolation but in relationships with other believers.

One of the reasons I turned on to Christ was because of others. I looked around and saw many people whom I trusted and respected believing in Jesus. Naturally, this is no basis for deciding the validity of religion, but it caused me to give religion a second look, being careful to try to understand it, and see what so many people saw in it. I found truth in the New Testament. What struck me the most was the idea of how God could be involved with us on earth in interpersonal encounter. . . .

All of what I have written is *my* answer. Does it work for others? I don't know. At the same time I often question my beliefs. There is much which could cause me to reject my faith, but I don't. . . . One of the things my faith has given me is optimism. I believe that things *will* get better and we *will* survive. I wish I could do more for the world, but I really don't know how. I am only one person in a world of many. My effect is small, but yet it is there. I hope that someday I will be able to do more.

In this (so far) religious success story, notice the creative tension between taking responsibility for himself and his beliefs and the need to derive inspiration from people he respects. There is another significant feature. He does not ask that other people be religious in the same way that he is, only that they be genuine and serious. That is true of the great majority of his contemporaries. They do not ask their elders to be like them, only that they be allowed to be themselves. In order to give the kind of good example that we have been discussing, adults do not have to change their own style of religious expression, worship, and prayer. But if their style is very different from that of the young, they must allow a new religious mode to emerge and take shape. This calls for patience, understanding, and a discriminating sense of what is essential and what is less important in doctrine and practice. Such awareness comes from reading, interaction, and continuing growth in religious comprehension. This is a lifelong task—a task that is crucial to our ability to guide our children and necessary for our own lifelong growth as Christians.

No religious identity, in any era, can be strong or even endure without a life of prayer. The skills that teenagers need to pursue a life of prayer are not easy to acquire. More is involved than "learning their prayers"; they must learn *to pray*. The rote recitation of prayer formulas learned from others is not something they want to do; it seems too mechanical, too lacking in spontaneity to be genuine. At first sight, the lack of formal prayer by the young seems to indicate a religious vacuum, but this is not the whole story. There is among them a remarkable receptivity to learning how to pray, when there is someone to teach them. At the moment, there seem to be far more potential pupils than effective teachers.

If your relationship with God is alive and well, your son or daughter will have a great introduction to a prayer life, since it is a truism that faith is not taught but caught. There is more involved here than teaching or learning. Relationships are more than ideas or words or even actions; they are the very stuff of life. When children are not only taught

108

to pray but see their parents pray, the chances are that God will be real to them and not just a rumor.

As your children get older, and their questions become more searching and harder to answer, take them seriously. Make religious learning experiences available to them in school or in parish programs. Read their religion books. Keep learning yourself. Subscribe to periodicals that offer help to parents in sharing faith with children. Enlist the aid of professionals and church volunteers, but don't turn everything over to them. You are still the most important person in the religious universe of your sons and daughters.

To Require Churchgoing or Not

Some parents have great difficulty handling this dilemma: Do I leave the kids on their own and perhaps be guilty of neglect, or do I insist on religious observance and risk alienating them from the very thing I want them to value? It is difficult to give an answer that applies to every family and every child. But as a general rule, parents have the right to oblige their growing children to go to church.

It would be nice if teenagers always did the right things without being told. They often do; but all of them, at one time or another, need to be made to do the things that must be done. If you tell your children that church attendance is optional, while school attendance and eating vegetables are obligatory, your message is coming through loud and clear: the mind and body *must* be cared for, but the cultivation of the soul is another matter. Maybe you didn't mean it that way, but that's the way it comes across. Of course, it goes without saying that if you tell *them* to go to church, then *you* had better be there yourself.

But don't just settle for putting your foot down. Find out if they have a real problem with church. Maybe the liturgy is celebrated in a lifeless, uninspired manner. Maybe you and they should go looking for a group and a celebration that try to respond to people's needs, specifically the needs of young people.

Remember, too, that time is running out on you if you still have to make them go to church. In a very few years they will be on their own. In the last analysis they are *free:* faith cannot be forced but must be freely accepted. When you have done all you can to encourage their religious growth, you have to know when to let go. The days are past when people practiced a religion all their lives because that is the way they were brought up and because it was expected of them. From now on, people are going to be Christian because that is their conviction and their choice, and they are making those choices with less and less social pressure.

Your teenagers are probably not ready to make such choices yet. But they are developing attitudes, values, and patterns of behavior that will eventually determine their future path. It may not be the same path that you have taken. When teenagers reject the faith and the church of their parents, it is hard for the parents to accept this deviation. But we must be no less respectful of their freedom than God is. And don't forget that there are many paths leading to our Father's house. Jesus speaks forcefully of those who belong to him, even though they do not know him, because they feed the hungry, clothe the naked, and shelter the homeless (Matt. 25:34-40). We all know people who do not share our faith, who perhaps have no explicit religious affiliation, but who are fine human beings— generous, compassionate, just. We do not think of these people as lost, but simply as different. We appreciate and even admire them. Where is it written that our children cannot be of their number?

Parents can do only so much. They must accept the limitations of religious upbringing. There is a real sense in which no one can "raise" a Christian. One must *become* a Christian by freely deciding to follow Jesus Christ within a community of his followers. We cannot program anyone to do that; even Jesus couldn't! We can prepare the soil, teach, train, encourage, and invite a child to faith. But there comes a time when he or she must choose to respond or not. And we must not be quick to judge them when they do not respond. They may be simply leaving for a time, to return after the storms of adolescence are past. Even if they do not come back, we do not know if they have really left. They may belong to the Lord in ways we do not know; indeed, they may be closer to him than we and many other believers are. After all, you know how much goodness is in your children; well, God knows them even better than you do. Leave them to him.

IN A NUTSHELL

Young people are open to religious faith, even hungry for it, but in ways different from their elders. Their images of God, their ways of praying, and their attitudes toward worship sometimes make them feel like outsiders in adult congregations. Not only are their expressions of faith distinctly different and often disturbing, but so is their approach to moral concerns. These differences cause many teenagers to look for God in places and groups outside the institutional church.

The next generation of Christians will have fewer cultural supports for their religious identity and will have to base their faith less on custom and more on conviction and choice. This more intensely personal relationship with God must be nourished by prayer and experiences of community. Such a relationship can hardly be imposed, so parents face the challenge of preparing their growing children for a freely chosen Christian commitment. In particular, parents can offer the kind of example that presents religion as an adult enterprise rather than an involvement reserved for children. But not all teenagers will be able or willing to make a commitment to Christianity, in which case parents must come to terms with the painful truth that their children may find ways to God different from their own.

DISCUSSION EXTENDERS

1. What have you seen in your children's behavior or that of other teenagers to support the contention that there is a new receptivity to religious faith among the young?

2. With which God do you feel more at home—the Creator-Lord-Judge or the Friend-Lover-Companion? Which vision has had more impact on your religious consciousness and style?

3. "Young people today have been spared some of the hangups of their forebears, but they are sometimes poorer in other ways." Explain how this statement does or does not apply to your children. To the wider church community.

4. Do you think sin and repentance are still operative concepts in the religious lives of teenagers and adults? Why or why not?

5. In a world where one salary no longer pays the bills for many families, is it reasonable to ask parents to give religious example by "investing time, talent, and energy in living out their faith"? How can working parents accomplish this?

6. What have you done to make prayer a part of your family's life together? How successful have you been?

7. Do you make your teenage children go to church? Should you? What do you think can be done to make church attendance more meaningful for them?

8. Are there any church drop-outs in your family? How do you come to terms with this disappointment?

9. In counseling hundreds of families whose grown children have decided to leave organized religion, Dale Francis has found these guidelines helpful:

Don't feel guilty.

Don't argue (but make clear your own firm convictions).

Don't say they "owe it to you."

Don't disown them.

Do stay close to them.

Do stay close to God.

Do leave a door open.

What do you find helpful and realistic about these guidelines?

10. What are the one or two most important religious values you want to hand on to your teenagers?

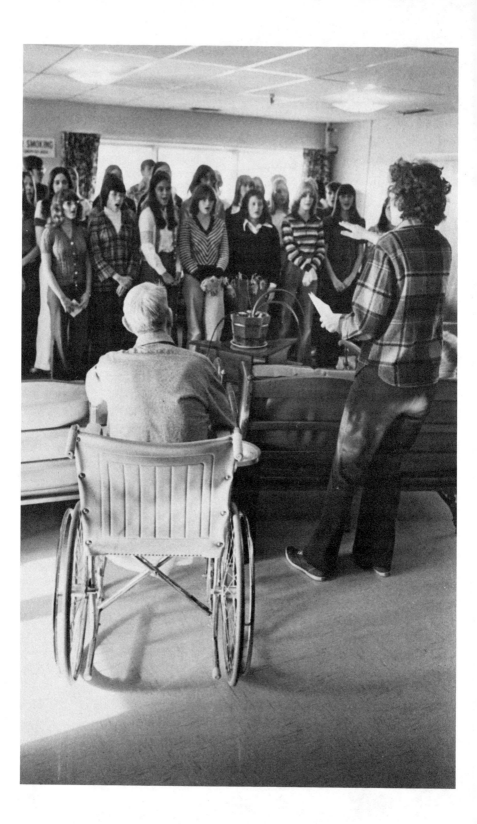

elp Wanted: Keeping the Faith

If young Christians are going to make the transition to adulthood without becoming religious casualties, they need all the help they can get. Parental influence and example—as just discussed—are paramount. But more is needed: experiences of Christian community, of prayer, and of worship—experiences that contribute positively to religious formation. Also, there should be moral development grounded in the kind of humanistic values that complement an authentically Christian vision of life.

Traditionally, the churches have provided helpers in the form of religion teachers. Sometimes these teachers are professionally trained in theology and religious education, but more often they are conscientious volunteers with limited formal training. They may teach in parish schools, but typically they teach in Sunday school or in released-time programs or in weekly after-school courses under parish auspices.

A new and increasingly important helper is emerging in the role of youth minister. This is someone whom parents concerned about the religious development of their children should know about. Youth ministers have long been prominent in some churches but have arrived somewhat later on

115

the scene in other communities. There is an obvious overlap between the two helpers: religion teachers are engaging in a form of ministry to youth; youth ministers often teach religion, though in less formal ways.

Actually, this raises a set of related questions:

- What kind of help can churches give to parents who take seriously their primary responsibility for the religious upbringing of teenage sons and daughters?
- How do we want our children to learn about God and Jesus and church?
- What are realistic religious expectations for teenagers when it is difficult just to bring them together, much less make them sit still and listen?
- When teenagers do listen, what do we want to say to them?
- What distinguishes an effective religion program from an ineffective one?

A close look at the emerging youth ministry places these questions in perspective and also helps parents understand what help they can expect from youth ministers.

Filling a Religious Vacuum

The blend of religious and social activities that is known as youth ministry has become a fixture in churches that do not run denominational high schools. In others, it is a relatively new arrival, having risen, phoenixlike, from the ashes of parish programs of religious instruction for public high school students. By the early 1970s, it had become clear that the students who had been dropping out of these programs in greater and greater numbers were not going to come back. All those brave and generous volunteers who were willing to teach religion had almost no one to teach. Among Catholic teenagers, reception of the sacrament of confirmation during junior high years became a signal for a mass exodus from religious schooling programs. There are some notable exceptions to this trend, especially in those churches and dioceses where confirmation is deferred until the later high school years. But to a great extent it could be said without exaggeration that, by the seventies, high school religious instruction outside of denominational schools was terminally ill.

Among the church people who cared about teenagers and wanted to fill the vacuum, the more imaginative stopped wringing their hands and decided to do something. They asked themselves: Is formal religious education, which teens no longer buy, the only thing we can offer them? Can't adolescents do anything within the church except take courses? Isn't ministry bigger than schooling? Out of the answers to these questions grew parish youth groups, which provide a focus for teen involvement in the life of the church community. Each of these groups has its own distinctive features, but certain common characteristics emerge from even a casual study of them. They provide a place for teenagers to go, make friends, and do things together. These activities are sometimes social and service oriented, sometimes educational, sometimes explicitly religious. The most successful groups are those that combine all three.

The formation and direction of youth groups call for skills beyond those required for a teacher. For several years now, the university programs that lead to master's degrees in religious education have included tracks and courses specializing in youth ministry. While this professionalization of youth workers is no panacea, it is a positive step in the right direction. Now, when a parish has lost contact with its teenagers and young adults, it can call upon professionals who know how to fill the vacuum.

A guiding principle of youth ministry is the need for young people to minister to one another. Many parish youth programs collapse or fail to fulfill their potential because adults don't want to, or don't know how to, turn over the reins of leadership to the young people themselves. There is always an important role for adults in these programs, but they fill it best when they stay in the background, providing encouragement and affirmation while the young leaders take responsibility for themselves and their peers. This youth-to-youth ministry, as it is called, is one of the most significant recent developments in the life of the church as it touches the young. What these young leaders may lack in theological sophistication and adult experience they make up in conviction, idealism, and enthusiasm. And they can reach their peers in ways adults never could.

A Piece of the Action

A crucial difference between the religious perception and style of the young and that of their elders is the felt need to have a piece of the action. Church members of an earlier time usually viewed religion as something that was done *to* and *for* them by ordained ministers and professional religious persons. Active leadership roles were reserved for clergy, religious, and professionals, while the laity saw themselves in passive roles of receptivity and fidelity. But today's young people are growing up in churches where these role expectations are changing. Ministries that were formerly the private preserve of the clergy are being turned over to the nonordained, either as a matter of principle or out of necessity. For example, in the past the new young curate could usually expect to inherit the parish youth activities. But in many of today's rectories there is no young curate. A professional youth minister or lay coordinator probably serves in his stead, and if the youth ministers know their stuff, they are training leaders among the youth group to minister to their peers.

These youth leaders are something of an elite, probably the next generation of lay leaders. Even the youngsters who do not aspire to leadership positions in the parish or community youth group are experiencing their faith not just as something to be accepted but as something to be *done*. When teens experience personal growth in these situations, some of which can be quite demanding, they come to see their faith not as a burden or an imposition but as a force of enrichment.

The development of these youth ministries has been uneven across the country. Some groups have succeeded in providing social activities but have been unable to get their members involved in liturgies and retreats. Others are still learning how to integrate their members into the life of the parish at large. Until they do this, they will be a kind of youth ghetto—in the parish but not of it.

However, as a knowledgeable observer like Michael Warren has noted, religious education suffered amidst a paradox of good intentions: "Youth catechesis in this country has practically died and it has happened in the past ten years. How did it happen? The irony is that it happened in the name of youth ministry." Warren's explanation is a revealing reminder that good intentions were not enough as fewer and fewer young people attended programs in religious education during the 1970s.

> Out of this situation of massive resistance to catechesis in once-a-week classes developed the concept of a comprehensive ministry to youth. . . . In an effective effort with youth, all the ministries had to be attended to: ministry of the word; ministry of worship; ministry of guidance, counsel, including education; and the ministry of healing. Further, many came to believe that for youth a principal ministry underlying and making possible the four major ministries was the ministry of friendship. . . .
>
> However, this development was accompanied by a problem, namely, that it did not go far enough. As a result, catechesis for teens has almost died out in many parts of the United States. Adults working by way of friendship with young people, relating effectively with them, do not always move actively enough to lead them to a deeper understanding of the meanings that bind the community together.[1]

A big problem, and one that will not go away, is the lack of skilled professionals to teach religion to children and

---

[1]Michael Warren, *Youth and the Future of the Church* (New York: Seabury Press, 1982), pp. 74-75.

youth. Although many graduate school programs offer master's degrees in religious education, their alumni are but a small fraction of those who teach the young. Sunday schools and parish instructional programs are usually staffed by unpaid volunteers. They are admirable, generous people, faced with the enormous challenge of relating faith and the gospel message to the everyday life of their students. Even when they are totally committed, the limitations imposed upon them by lack of time, lack of continuity, and inadequate facilities and resources often prevent them from successfully meeting this challenge.

The parochial school situation is somewhat better, since instruction is more frequent, more structured, and better organized; but even here there are grave difficulties. In the elementary schools, it is often taken for granted that everyone on the faculty, with or without formal credentials, will teach religion in their classes. Even in high schools, many administrators fail to apply the same standards of professionalism in hiring or appointing religion teachers that they follow in staffing other departments. The notion dies hard that "anyone can teach religion."

Can't Anyone?

Does an adult Christian have to possess special credentials in order to share faith with the young? Are we over-stressing the role of professionals in religious formation in church-related schools? Doesn't this stress undermine the primacy of the parental role in faith formation?

These objections are reasonable. It is important not to exaggerate the impact of formal religious instruction. The old saying is still true: Faith is caught rather than taught. There is no substitute for personal witness and example. But look at the other side of the coin. Youngsters grow up today in a culture that not only fails to support religious faith but is, in many ways, hostile to it. The world view, the vision of life, and the values portrayed on television, in the movies, in music, and in other media are often far removed from the gospel vision and values. Adults are so accustomed to moving in and out of these separate worlds that they hardly notice. Children become confused and need wise, experienced guides to find their way through the confusion. Remember the students, referred to in Chapter 3, who said that Zacchaeus would have been better off if he had not met Jesus, since his conversion cost him a comfortable income? That is only one instance in a growing mass of evidence that, in late twentieth-century America, Christianity is becoming more and more countercultural.

Changing Times

The past alliance between church and family has been undermined. Father and mother, grandfather and grandmother once had a unified attitude toward the church, its values, and its authority. They accepted and respected the church, and they forcefully communicated their feelings and beliefs to their children. It was a family-church alliance that was common in the early decades of this century. But no more, as this succinct description points out:

> As the family changed, and as new influences came into the family, the impact of the church began to wane. The way of life represented by a long religious tradition began to be neglected. It would be too much to say that the church was opposed. It wasn't opposition that began to appear. It was, first of all, a weaning or separation. With all this moving around, with so many new stimuli coming into the family, there was a gradual but continuing separation of family life from frequent church and Sunday school participation. This meant a decrease in the quantity and quality of contact with religious traditions and their emphasis upon values. This should not be underestimated as a factor in today's world of confusion and apathy.[2]

---

[2]Louis Raths, Merrill Harmin, and Sidney Simon, *Values and Teaching* (Columbus, Ohio: Charles E. Merrill, 1966), p. 19.

This is where professional religious educators come in. They should have a grasp not only of their religious tradition, its teachings, and its theology, but also of the surrounding culture, that larger world within which faith must be lived. They should be well grounded in education—not only the skills and methods that make for good teaching, but also the psychology of the learner. They must understand how children grow and learn. In particular, they must know how to relate religion to a child's cognitive and emotional development. They must take into account the adolescent's ability to relate to religious stories and concepts and the process of arriving at personal conviction and commitment. This involves an understanding of the way youngsters think and feel about right and wrong, about sin and guilt. The competent religious educator must be something of a generalist rather than a specialist in order to do justice to these many dimensions of growing up.

Is it unreasonable to demand so much of professional religious educators? Not in a pluralistic society like this one, where Christianity rubs shoulders in a free market with all kinds of competing faiths and value systems. It is unrealistic to expect all religion instructors to master all these skills. Certainly the unpaid volunteers, who will always be the mainstay of church education networks, cannot be expected to fit all these strings to their bows. But directors and coordinators of religious education should be expected to keep pace with developments in these fields and provide leadership and assistance to the nonprofessional volunteers. Church-related schools should demand a similar level of professional competence among those who teach religion for a living. It is hard to understand why amateurism is tolerated in the teaching of this one subject in those very schools which claim that religious affiliation is their distinctive characteristic and religious formation their top priority.

Still, some may wonder: Why are professional skills suddenly so necessary? Didn't people learn their faith as children without all this sophisticated educational apparatus? Indeed they did, but in a much simpler world where there were fewer voices, fewer choices, fewer conflicting signals competing for attention and allegiance. It was a time when children could be indoctrinated, when a religious identity could be established without critical thinking, without student-centered, open-ended discussion, without conscious choice.

Those days are gone forever. Today's youth live in a world of choice, alternatives, and variety. Their world is permeated with stimuli, information, fad and fashion, celebrities, competing role models, simplistic ideologies. They have so many places to turn, so many directions to follow, so many voices to heed that they are confused. Although not blurted out in straightforward, direct terms, one question hounds them, as it has always hounded the young: *What do I believe?*

Fortunate are those teenagers who have adults who are able and willing to help them answer that question. Many adult believers are ready to tell them what they *should* believe, or what they themselves believe, or what they perceive their church as telling its members what they should believe. This is all well and good but who is going to answer the inquisitive, skeptical adolescent who asks *why?* Too few adults are ready to take these questions seriously or to try to answer them honestly. All too often they have not faced these questions themselves or taken the trouble to find answers on their own. So they understandably fear the open-ended, unstructured dialogues that young inquirers want and need.

Facing Their Questions

Teenagers have questions they did not ask as children. Why aren't other religions as good as ours? How do we know that? Can people be saved without belonging to our church? And if they can, why should we belong? How do we know that God exists? Is it all a matter of opinion? Don't we just have to follow our conscience? And so on and so on.

Youngsters who do not attend church-related schools have limited opportunities to discuss these questions, so they may seldom or never ask them out loud. Then, too, the anti-intellectualism so characteristic of American religiosity discourages such inquiries and reinforces the popular impression that religious faith is an arbitrary, unquestioning option based simply on emotion and is not to be examined the way other commitments are. Even in church-related schools, students are often surprised when competent religious educators encourage critical thinking and open discussion. But it is important that these educators challenge young minds and try to produce thinking as well as feeling Christians.

> Theology in the classroom should not be primarily at the service of the Church but should be an open search for truth. Yet such a theology would ultimately be of service to the Church because it would give intellectual rigor to the questioning already taking place among young people inside and in many cases outside the Church. Such a questioning in our schools, far from being dangerous, is invigorating; the only thing which is dangerous and depressing is an unquestioning and mindless acceptance or rejection of Christianity.[3]

Invigorating educational experiences can be produced and managed effectively only by competent, confident teachers who relish open-ended inquiries from students. It takes time and effort and continued study to become such a teacher, but it is worth the trouble. What helps most of all is to be a believer who acknowledges doubts, who is not afraid to raise questions, who tries to think critically and to be a religiously adult person. Such persons need not fear the questions and challenges of the young, for they have already faced them in their own lives.

It is never easy to pass on to children, faithfully and effectively, the essentials of religious belief. Well-meaning adults can have a very limited grasp of the Christian

---

[3]Geoffrey Turner, "Theology in the Classroom," *The Tablet*, London, February 28, 1981, p. 208.

message. For their part, children are limited in their ability to understand what is taught. Sometimes adults try to teach too much too soon; sometimes they teach too little or in a superficial manner that sells children short. Even when childhood instruction is done well, there are new tasks and challenges as young people pass through adolescence toward adulthood. If their religious growth is to keep pace with their increasing maturity, they must appropriate their faith in new ways. Becoming an adult believer is a formidable undertaking. Attitudes of dependence and docility must be integrated with such grown-up qualities as independence and responsibility. Otherwise the onset of young adulthood will be seen as a time to throw off the shackles of a religious training that threatens to keep them children. There are too many people who feel they have outgrown religion, and too many who refuse to grow in the name of religion.

The Alternatives

To appreciate the kind of religious formation that we are espousing, it helps to consider some other ways that have been tried and found wanting. The first is a fideistic approach, designed to elicit assent by stifling inquiry and repressing doubt. Depending on the particular Christian denomination, it may have taken the form of biblical fundamentalism or of ecclesiastical authoritarianism. The former appeals to an infallible book; the latter, to infallible churchmen. Both have always appealed to those people, young or old, who were too lazy or too timid to think for themselves. They have exercised a perennial attraction for those who hunger for the security that comes with a black-and-white world shorn of complexity and devoid of risk.

There will always be a certain number of adolescents willing to forego critical thinking and to buy security at the expense of intellectual independence. They will remain comfortable with this arrangement just so long as they remain faithful to the implicit commitment to refrain from thinking. This phenomenon is found in its most extreme form in the young members of religious cults, where manipulation is blatant and the loss of identity disturbingly evident. The religious fundamentalists and authoritarians will doubtless object to being placed in the same category with cult leaders. To do them justice, it must be admitted that they have done much less harm and often quite a bit of good. But they are brothers and sisters under the skin, offering a religious identity on the condition that their followers sacrifice their individuality.

The second form that religious education has sometimes taken grew out of an overreaction to the excesses just described. In attempting to avoid indoctrinating the young, the people who went this route sometimes taught too little. Laudable efforts to inculcate attitudes of honesty, compassion, tolerance, and justice failed to integrate moral concerns with authentic doctrine and tradition. Such efforts produced a vague humanism loosely associated with religious concerns, resulting in what could only be described as religious illiteracy. Thus young people emerged from such educational experiences without the knowledge and the skills necessary for meaningful participation in church life.

No Shortcuts

Like it or not, there is no shortcut, no easy road to helping young people evolve a personal religious identity. This is especially true in an era of religious and cultural pluralism, when faith can no longer depend on habit or custom but must be built on personal conviction and free choice. In today's church-related high schools, the current emphases on personal appropriation, on attention to and respect for feelings and emotions, and on a student-centered approach to learning are all good in themselves. But they run the risk of intellectual laziness and of creating the impression that religion is a matter not of truth but of taste. There is plenty of evidence that this impression is widespread among young Christian adults.

During these formative years, young people need adult example and personal experience of friendship, community, celebration, idealism, and service. They need to be

126

ministered to by their peers as well as by their elders; and some of them are capable, with encouragement and support, of exercising that ministry themselves. It would be most desirable for them to receive the kind of religious education that challenges minds as well as hearts. If parents invest in education at church-related schools, they should settle for nothing less.

Something less, though, is what they are likely to get if they do not know what they are looking for. And even if they get the kind of religious formation that we have been advocating, the results will depend not only on the young person's free response but also on the religious growth of the parents themselves. Michael Warren has perhaps said it best:

> Fostering their own religious growth is what enables parents—indeed, any adults—to be with young people in religiously significant ways. In my judgment, knowing how to be with youth in religiously significant ways is perhaps the crucial knowledge for anyone who would hope to invite them more deeply into the mystery revealed in Jesus.[4]

Fortunately, there are large numbers of young people around today who have met the real Jesus, who have put him at the center of their lives, and who are sharing him with others. They are the hope of churches suffering a crisis of identity. Yes, young people seem to be staying away in large numbers, but those who remain give promise of a bright future. Different from the past? Definitely. Better? Maybe.

---

[4]Warren, *Youth and the Future of the Church*, p. 44.

IN A NUTSHELL

"Knowing their religion" is just one of the needs of young people that must be met if they are to take their place in the church. Youth ministry includes teaching religion and much more; it should provide experiences of community, worship, service, and youth-to-youth leadership. Failure to do so may accelerate the already disturbing rate at which young people are leaving the church.

Special training and skills are needed both for youth ministers and religious educators. Although volunteers will always form the backbone of the churches' efforts to socialize the young, the need for professional leaders has increased as the cultural supports for religious identity fade away in a pluralistic society.

Young people's questioning should be encouraged and taken seriously. The teaching of religion should challenge the mind as well as the heart. It should aim not at indoctrination but at the kind of dialogue that promotes free decision and mature commitment. Such education, when reflected in the lives of parents and other adults, not only helps keep teenagers in the church but prepares them for leadership.

DISCUSSION EXTENDERS

1. What would you like your parish, church, and school to provide in helping with the religious development of your teenage children?

2. What made a difference to you when you were growing up and developing your religious commitment? Which experiences? Which adults? What did they say and do?

3. How do you compare the religious freedom of your children with the freedom you had while growing up? What are the significant differences?

4. What have you done to help your teenagers experience their faith "not just as something to be accepted but as something to be *done*"?

5. How do you view the need for professional religious educators as opposed to the need for personal witness and example? Do you agree that the changing times have created a situation that demands the skills of professional religious educators?

6. What standards would you apply in evaluating the religious programs offered in your parish and school?

7. What counts most in the way parents and teachers discuss religion with teenagers?

8. What steps have you taken to foster continued religious growth? Do you agree with Michael Warren that this is what enables parents "to be with young people in religiously significant ways"?

9. Is there a youth-to-youth ministry in your church? What can be done to encourage young leaders to take this responsibility? How can they reach their peers in ways that adults cannot?

10. What would you say if a teenager asked you what you believed, *really* believed?

CHAPTER 8

Coming Full Circle: Parents Themselves

The more we try to understand young people, the more we find out about adults. Any attempt to deal effectively with adolescents inevitably comes full circle. We start out by asking questions about teenagers and end up with questions about ourselves.

While young people have been in the forefront of our concern throughout this book, we as parents and other caring adults had to be included to complete the picture. When we wondered aloud what our children want, we had to ask ourselves, What do *we* want? If youngsters seem afraid of commitment, wary of ideals, lacking in enthusiasm, what about us? Just how different are we? When the going gets tough, do we get going or just go along? What kind of role models are we for a generation that sometimes seems ready to settle for a narrow slice of life?

We are rightly concerned about our growing children's experiences with drugs, including alcohol. And we must do all we reasonably can to help them deal with this threat. But honesty compels us to examine our own liquor cabinets and medicine chests to measure our dependence on, or freedom from, the artificial fix. The young learn from us many a lesson that we do not want to teach.

Their experiments with sex worry us, and with good reason. But the more we try to encourage responsible attitudes toward sexuality, the more we are compelled to examine our own convictions, values, and feelings. If the young are confused and misled, they have picked up confusion from their elders—not just from the corrupters and exploiters, but also from the "good guys." When caring adults are able to accept their sexuality in a positive, joyous spirit that can counsel restraint without repression or false guilt, they earn the kind of credibility for which finger-wagging is no substitute.

When we wonder about the religious beliefs and practices of adolescents, we have to probe the depth and seriousness of adult religious commitment. No discussion of teenagers' church attendance is complete without an investigation into the motives of adult churchgoers. Our consideration of youthful religiosity requires us to take another look at ourselves. What do *we* believe? What does our faith do for us? What difference does God make in our lives? What do we offer our children besides words?

These considerations are not designed to put us on the defensive or to absolve our children of responsibility just because parents sometimes fail. We are not required to be perfect before we can challenge or discipline them. But the conclusion is inescapable that adult leadership is a crucial factor in the growth of the young. The intent here is not to lay one more guilt trip on parents, but to make certain they do not underestimate their own influence.

Parents as Influentials

In the give-and-take of teen years—with the real and inflated crises, with the emotional and psychological peaks and valleys—parents do their best and say their prayers. They realize that there are no guarantees, even for those parents who try to build walls around their youngsters. But no matter what parents do—whether they are autocratic or democratic, overbearing or easygoing, repressive or permissive—they have an incredible influence over their sons and daughters, both intended and unintended.

Even discerning parents are surprised by the signs of influence they have over their children. The obvious influences are not as important as the effects upon outlook, ways of dealing with others, fundamental views of life. To illustrate parental influence, we collected responses from college juniors and seniors whose memories of the teen years are still fresh. At the same time, they can look back with new perspective, particularly now that they have the much greater independence of college students on their own. Anyone with a teenage son or daughter will wonder while reading these answers how his or her own teenager will answer the question, How did your parents influence you as a teenager?

> My parents influenced me by telling me what *not* to do, based on their own experiences. As a teenager, I could never understand it when they said, "I know what's right and wrong because I was once a teenager also." As a teenager, I could not relate to this because we came from two different generations. But, as I look back, they were right. Everything that they did, all the mistakes which they made, they tried to pass this information on to me so that I would not do the same things. In other words, they tried to pass their knowledge of life on to me.

> As a teenager my parents most influenced me in their control over my actions and in their support. My parents were strict in my high school years and asked who I was to be with, what time I was expected home. They kept close tabs on my daily activities. They disallowed any activity towards drinking or drugs and made it hard for me to try them without getting caught. They would wait up at night or else I had to wake them when I came home. They also respected me though and gave me enough independence to partake in activities I chose. When I acted responsibly, I gained extra privileges. In school I received

good grades and was given special gratification. My parents were generous with the car. Because they also supported me so well and were so loving, I developed a feeling of obligation towards them. Guilt often made me remain obedient.

Everything my parents did had some influence on me. In fact, today most of my friends say I'm a young version of my mother. The two of them were Italian Catholic immigrants who came to America over thirty years ago. With them came the typical "Immigrant Dream." Because of that Dream they impressed on me the idea that an education is absolutely necessary in order to make it. They also emphasized being independent and hardworking because if something ever happened you could always rely on yourself. While today I may see that some of these ideals can wear thin, I still see that my parents' influence and ideas have made me value their ideals and make them my own. All in all, I think it's a pretty neat idea that I'm sort of carrying on the tradition. It's even neater that now that I'm older I see that they were basically right.

Through my father's mistake, I will never stay with a job or career that I dislike. I think it is more important that you like what you are doing than to worry about how much you are making. The pressures of a job that he did not like have made my father miserable at times. Through the influence of both parents I have learned to listen to people and really respect their opinion. However, I have also learned to take pride in myself and never let anyone or any situation get the best of me. My personality comes from my mother and my values from my father.

My parents, particularly my father, were very autocratic. I wasn't given a chance to be independent. They were always at my back. They gave my friends hell. They didn't like my boyfriend and they embarrassed me a lot. I think because of that I'm not very confident about how I am and what I can do. I always think the worst of myself. But I am slowly building up my confidence and self-esteem since I am no longer living at home with them. I don't resent them. They didn't know about child psychology and those things. Now I understand their point of view. And we're the best of friends now.

My parents affected me in that they controlled my life through using guilt. If I wanted to do something or go somewhere they didn't want me to, I was made to feel I was embarrassing or upsetting them. That was enough to stop me. I never drank or used drugs because I was afraid of making a fool out of myself and thereby embarrassing myself and my family. There was a pretense of letting me make my own decisions or having my own opinion, but most of the time I adopted their attitudes because any less displeased them. College has been a tough experience for me because I am finally having to make my own decisions and for a while I didn't know what I thought. But I am beginning to become my own person, a part of them, but really myself.

My parents influenced me not so much by what they said but by what they didn't say. They never pressured me on topics under "don'ts"—no sex, drugs, drink. Rather, they took it for granted that I "didn't"; they trusted me that I "wouldn't." The key word is *trust,* and that shows mutual respect. I never had a curfew yet I was home at a reasonable hour. I drank but was never totally "ripped." The reason: my parents trusted me enough to respect myself. I didn't want to hurt them or let them down.

My parents' influence is something that's hard to describe. At the time, I wanted no influence whatsoever! Any advice, etc., was rejected—I wanted to do things on my own. My parents played up to this in a way because now I realize everything they did *was for me* yet they let me think I was "independent." Actually I'm starting to understand already some of those statements like "Someday you'll understand." Someday has arrived because now, more than ever, I *am* independent. I can see things they did for me as being (most of the time) "for my own good." I don't know if this is making any sense. What I'm trying to say is they taught me to be independent while still letting me depend on them. There were times I hated them and wished they'd mind their own business. Now I see that *I am* their business, but I also see that they and their lives are my business too. And this is ok. You can be independent *while* being into someone else's life, *while* being dependent on them for certain things. I am not the big shot I thought I was, but neither are they the tyrants I thought they were.

Only recently, these young men and women were teenagers. They have left those years behind, but not fully. Their responses reflect joint experiences in the growing-up years when their lives and the lives of their parents were intertwined. Parents must look inward to imagine the answers they would like their own teenagers to give. When your child is immersed in the teen years, you are—in effect—shaping the answer.

The WHY and the WHAT FOR

This book has tried to help parents without oversimplifying their role or exaggerating their power. We would like to put a warning sign on simplistic "how-to" formulas that tend to relieve parents of the responsibility of looking not only at their teenagers but at themselves as well. Parents need more than tips or strategies that make parenting seem like learning to hit a better backhand, grow a better lawn, make more on the stock market, earn more, waste less, and retire happily ever after.

What parents need is *why* and *what for*. At meetings, lectures, and discussions, the parents' enthusiastic response to this approach shows that they want to understand the many and varied influences on their children. Parents also realize that they function most effectively in the parental role when they understand themselves. For, after all, parents are not just authority figures or behavior managers. They are carriers of values who, as their children grow older, must lead more by persuasion and example and less by threats and commands.

When parents come looking for help, they begin by asking questions like, "What do we do when the kids . . . ?" These are "how-to" questions. What parents need first is to understand why the kids do what they do, what they really want, what is at stake in a tug-of-war between old and young. These are the "why" questions behind the "how-to" questions. If this book has helped parents to understand not only their children but also the world we live in and the forces that mold us all, then it has already started to work.

As noted earlier, teenagers have won most of their battles—to be taken seriously, to be listened to, to be given greater freedom. But they don't seem to be enjoying the fruits of their victory. They have less pain than in the past when they felt outrage, hostility, resentment. But they also seem to experience less pleasure, have less fun. Perhaps they sense that greater freedom is followed by the challenge of *freedom for what?* They need help with the *what*.

The task of learning to deal with freedom has been complicated by three little words that are heard more and more among teenagers. They also underlie many disagreements between the generations in the family. The words are waved like a banner by teenagers and often viewed as a form of graffiti by parents. The words reach to the depths of moral theology and also skim the surface of do-goodism.

The misleadingly simple words are *Follow your conscience.*

Authoritarians, in times past, avoided this issue by laying down the law to teenagers. They, in effect, told teenagers to follow the rules as strictly laid down by those in authority. Time and cultural circumstances have undermined this response to increased teenage freedom. Everyone, except authoritarian holdouts, realizes that such an approach does not work in the long run. Even in the short run, its results are precarious, typically producing grudging acquiescence and lip service. It ignores the fact that there is a long life after adolescence—a life characterized by freedom. The college students quoted above leapt into that freedom right after high school.

But we do not advocate the other extreme, either. The reaction to yesterday's widespread authoritarianism produced a hands-off policy. Concerned, responsible, committed Christian parents and educators hesitated to confront teenagers and were reluctant to interfere with their freedom. They saw confrontation as a way of turning off youngsters and creating a backlash. They saw telling youngsters what to think and do as a violation of freedom and as an obstacle to independent thinking. Such adults tended to become worried bystanders hoping for the best.

Being a bystander not only goes against the spirit of this book; it goes against the grain of responsible adult Christians. Helping others to grow does not mean denying our own strong commitments and convictions. It means standing up for them without imposing them on others. Helping others involves standing up for personal beliefs and caring enough for teenagers to let them know what the committed Christian stands for. It involves a living, learning, loving dialogue between concerned adults and teenagers. It involves a set of interrelated attitudes:

- I respect your views and take them seriously.
- I value your willingness to share your views with me.
- I treasure your trust that I will take your views seriously.
- I will never reject you, but that does not mean I will automatically accept your views. I'm certain you would say the same.

138

- I have my own convictions and commitments, and they are important to me. I would do them and you a disservice if I did not make them clear to you.
- Here's where I stand and why . . .

This constellation of attitudes does not produce instant or complete agreement. Nor does it produce applause. But relations with teenagers built on that foundation elicit mutual trust and respect. In the process, teenagers confront the truism that following your conscience does not give you license to *do your own thing*—regardless. A conscience is formed by thinking through alternatives in terms of values and standards. It emerges after listening to, and weighing, voices of authority, experiences, and expertise. It is serious business.

Ten Guidelines for Christian Parents

Time and again, parents ask for guidelines in facing the challenge of helping teenage sons and daughters develop into self-directed Christians. That is not the time to respond with glib remedies or foolish guarantees, not the occasion for promising, "If you do this . . ." But it is appropriate to offer guidelines that can be applied to particular sons and daughters in the particular circumstances of their families.

So we conclude by presenting ten guidelines which parents can draw upon in "writing" their own handbook for parenting teenagers.

1. Be firm, but not rigid.

What counts is the spirit of the law, not the letter. It is the difference between exercising authority and being authoritarian. The authoritarian parent is unable to listen and unwilling to compromise. Inflexible, unbending, such a parent seems unable to see the world in the concrete and his or her teenager in the flesh. By contrast, the firm parent is reasonable and loving, attentive to the needs of the individual teenager and alert to the consequences of actions and responses of *both* parent and child. For example, when a teenager comes home half an hour after the specified time, it is appropriate to confront him or her about the lateness, but not sensible to impose punishment. A home is not a military garrison.

2. Be vigilant, but respect teen privacy.

At their sensitive time of development, teenagers are struggling to establish their own individuality. They need to feel that parents respect their personal boundaries. They are outraged when adults violate their territory, and are desolate when they feel they have no private retreat. Then they literally do not have a place of their own, something that is crucial to the process of growing up. Certainly, parents must keep track of what teenagers do, where they go, and with whom. They should be aware of what goes on at the parties and who is there. It is necessary to be on the alert for signs of problems in the way teenagers behave, how they do in school, and how they function in the family. If there are strong reasons to suspect that teenagers are involved in dangerous behavior, then their right to privacy yields to the parental responsibility to protect their safety. Concern for their welfare is different from intrusive curiosity, which invariably backfires. A prying parent makes a secretive teenager.

3. Respect individuality.

Teenagers often like to flout the conventions and thereby manage to make the wrong impression at the wrong time, particularly when parents want to show them off. The more teenagers mature, the more likely they will go their own way, form different opinions, and resist fitting preconceived molds. Teenagers want to feel that they can be themselves and be accepted, even when they do not conform to the conventions.

A poignant plea on behalf of letting teenagers be themselves was expressed by a college senior who recalled how as a teenager she "hated" her mother and "loved" her father.

I hated my mother and loved my father. It stemmed from the fact that I was the baby of eight in my family. The oldest two were girls and the next five were boys, so I naturally grew up being a tomboy. Well, my mother wanted me to be a lady and domesticated baby girl like my much older sisters. However, I couldn't be like that. I had maintained my femininity, but I wasn't interested in staying in and learning how to make homemade bread or playing the piano. I wanted to play sports all year long: hockey in the fall, basketball in the winter, softball in the spring. I was never home in high school before 7 P.M. and always missed dinner. My mother despised my playing sports! On the other hand, my father used to get out of work early to come and watch my games and all of my brothers would crowd into the gym with their friends, screaming and yelling for me. I loved my father and brothers for this. But as much as they would encourage me and try to convince my mother that she would enjoy the games if she went, she refused to. I hated her because I thought that the one thing I loved most she hated me for. If it weren't for my father, I would have run away from home many times. He loved me dearly because I was his baby girl and I made him so proud! Yet, my mother and he constantly bickered about me. I always felt hatred toward my mother because of how she treated me during my high school years, and it is only recently that we started understanding and loving each other.

4. Love teens unconditionally and make sure they know it.

The love between parent and child is unique. It does not come about because two human beings meet at a crucial intersection in their lives. Nor does it emerge from talking, working, or simply being together, nor from discovering a kindred soul. The love of parent for child *is*—no questions asked, no strings attached. That unconditional love is the rock on which each child builds a personal life. The love is a given. Parents love their children not because of what they do but because they *are*. Yet parents can seem to wrap their love with many strings—getting good grades, making the team, winning, achieving, succeeding. Such conditions confuse the underlying message of love: *I, the parent, love my child no matter what he or she does.* For Christians, the only one who unequivocally makes that statement in its fullest meaning is God. God's love is what makes each human being count, each person special. Parental love mirrors divine love.

5. Ask more from life than comfort and security.

Teenagers need parents with ideals and aims that look beyond only taking care of No. 1. Parents then become role models as responsible and responsive Christians. Bluntly speaking, anyone wanting only comfort and security in life is ineligible to be a Christian—or a humanist, for that matter. As Eric Fromm has pointed out, "The respect for life, that of others as well as one's own, is the concomitant of the process of life itself and a condition of psychic health. . . . No healthy person can help admiring, and being affected by, manifestations of decency, love, and courage; for these are the forces on which his own life rests."[1]

In a pre-Christmas issue bulging with advertisements for luxury items, the *New Yorker* magazine published a cartoon with a strong message poking fun at the all-for-me mentality. It showed the devil holding his pitchfork and flanked by two leering helpers as he greets a new set of arrivals. He is advising them on what it is like in hell: "You'll find there's no right or wrong here. Just what works for *you*." As for parents, they must beware. Teenagers are watching.

---

[1]Erich Fromm, *Man for Himself: An Inquiry into the Psychology of Ethics* (New York: Holt, Rinehart and Winston, 1947), pp. 225-26.

6. Cultivate a relationship with God.

Christians celebrate a transcendent dimension in their lives. They have a relationship with God that goes beyond religious rituals and conventions. The relationship is based on awareness of the presence of God and the power of divine love. As the First Epistle of John proclaims, "We love because God first loved us" (1 John 4:19). Christians pray to celebrate life and God in their lives. They do not merely recite prayers; they listen as well as talk to God. Parents who pray do not need to carry signs telling teenagers that their mother and father are Christians. The parents themselves are the signs.

7. Keep growing in faith.

For Christian parents, faith is an open-ended affair. They are open to new ideas and are always learning new facets of faith. They constantly discover new ways of worshiping, new approaches toward personal prayer, new experiences of community. This is the opposite of the attitude that says, "I worked it all out long ago and that's the way it is and will be, for me, forever. Amen." Openness and growth in faith are reflected by a spirit of optimism and a sense of discovery. Teenagers whose parents continue to grow in faith receive a powerful message: Religion is a lifelong affair. There is faith after high school.

8. Put the accent on substance rather than style.

Adults often look in a rearview mirror when they deal with current teen styles in dress, music, movies, modes of studying and learning, forms of socializing, ways of looking at the future. In particular, parents sometimes hound their teenagers with questions about what they are going to be "when they grow up." It upsets many parents when their sons and daughters do not have a definitive answer about their career plans. For teenagers, it's a different world—with many more options and much less clarity, much more change and much less certainty. Teenagers back away from pinning themselves down about the future. What is essential is that teenagers find a constructive role to play in society, that they pursue work that satisfies their personal aptitude and interests, and that they make a contribution as competent, functioning adults. What counts is who teenagers *are*. Their particular way of confronting present and future comes second.

9. Work at communication.

It takes two to communicate, and against that barrier many a good intention crashes in the world of family communication. In pinpointing the pivotal role of communications, psychologist Sven Wahlroos has observed that in the "vast majority" of families in conflict "the main reason for the discord is simply that the consciously felt love and the good intentions harbored by the family members are not *communicated* in such a way that they are recognized."[2]

How can we communicate? The temptation is to turn immediately to words as magical solutions. Actually, in face-to-face communication, researchers have demonstrated that as much as 80 percent of the meaning is transmitted by nonverbal language. Communication in the family takes many forms. Besides body language, facial expressions, and tone of voice, family history gets into the transmission. Family members have long memories and they remember what words actually meant in the past. They also have personal inventories of the actions that have spoken much louder than any words.

Actually, communication never stops in the family. It ranges from seating arrangements at the table to allotment of space in the home, from nicknames to jokes, from gift giving to assignment of household duties. Messages continually flood the family, including the messages that parents are trying to disguise or hide.

Timing is particularly important with teenagers. They are not ready to communicate on command what is important to them. Nor is anyone for that matter. Often teenagers communicate indirectly by talking about other

---

[2]Sven Wahlroos, *Family Communication* (New York: Macmillan, 1974), p. viii.

people and other situations. Their behavior speaks volumes, and sometimes their silence speaks loudest of all. When discussions emerge naturally—and those are the meaningful discussions—the parent is called upon to display humility. The know-it-all parent does not discuss; he or she tells and in the telling cannot even be sure that the message was received as intended.

A final piece of advice on communication: when all other forms of communication with teenagers fail, try listening.

10. Honor teen needs.

The most urgent needs and the most pressing problems of teenagers differ from those of parents. Teenage priorities center on affirmation, support, encouragement. They need to feel that they are normal, and they desperately need friends. Loneliness is a particular threat to teenagers. They fear rejection, isolation, being left out. They struggle for acceptance. Meanwhile, they are learning to deal with their emotional and physical needs. In all this, parents can do only so much. Often they sit patiently on the sidelines, hoping and praying as they watch sons and daughters grow up, something the young must do on their own. Teenagers are immersed in a burning present. Parents have a shifting focus: yesterday's child, today's teenager, tomorrow's adult.

The bottom line for this set of guidelines remains what it always has been: practice what you preach. At some point, sons and daughters will recall their teen years and apply that test, as one college senior did in the following excerpt. Which parent would you want to be remembered as?

> My mother practiced what she preached. We always knew where she stood—fantastic person. Taught me how to really love—still does.
>
> My father was a hypocrite with one set of standards for the family and one for everyone else. Didn't practice what he preached. Unfortunately, no one in the family liked him. He seemed two-faced. He never said anything to us.

145

We never knew what he was thinking. He ruined any possible relationships between his family and himself.

I think it's obvious how they influenced me, one over the other.

As parents and helping adults, we have—finally—to look to our own selves. We can help teenagers become responsible Christians, provided we ourselves are free. Free from the kind of fear that stifles idealism and leaves no room for dreams. Free from slavish, unthinking conformity to convention. Free from chemical fixes. Free from fear of our own bodies and our own feelings. Free to believe, to risk letting God all the way into our lives, to make commitments and live up to them. A large order, certainly. But if that is what we want for our children, we have to lead the way. There is no guarantee that they will follow, but at least we will have tried. No one—not even God—could ask for more.

We do not want to lead our children's lives for them, but we would like to make a difference. How much? Not so much that they are carbon copies, but enough to influence them positively as they become their own unique, self-directed, best selves. Then we are helping to prepare the young to live not in our past but in their future.

IN A NUTSHELL

Parents of teenagers experience growing up a second time. First time, they managed it themselves. Second time, they experience it as ally, authority figure, friend, critic, guide, resource aide, loving mother or father. It is never the same from one generation to the next or even from one child to the next, but the shared experience is humanly fulfilling in the deepest sense.

If shared deeply and conscientiously, the growing-up process renews parents by directing them not only outwardly toward teenagers and their world but also inwardly toward themselves as individuals. Looking at the child as a reflection of themselves brings self-examination. It is an enriching experience for the basic reason that the "unexamined life is not worth living." It is an incomparable human experience of passing on life and commitment to life—of building the future, a thoroughly Christian act of optimism.

DISCUSSION EXTENDERS

1. When was the last time you sat down and listened to your teenage son or daughter? What did you learn about yourself as a parent?

2. What traits of yours do you see reflected in your teenager?

3. How do you think your teenage son or daughter views you? How would he or she describe you? Try checking your guess with his or her description. How close did you come?

4. Does your son or daughter feel free to speak candidly to you? What can you do to encourage candid discussions with your teenager?

5. How would you like your children's life to be different from yours? What are you doing to steer them in the desired direction?

6. Are you an optimist or a pessimist? What about your children? How can an attitude of optimism or pessimism affect one's life?

7. If your teenage son or daughter were asked, "What is the greatest influence your parents have had on you?" what do you hope he or she would say? What do you think he or she would actually believe?

8. How do you think your children would fare in life if they lived by the words *Follow your conscience?* Where do you stand on the continuum from "authoritarian" to "worried bystander"?

9. Is your relationship with your teenager built on the attitudes listed on pages 138-39? What could you do to encourage mutual trust and respect?

10. How would you evaluate your practice of each of the ten guidelines presented in this chapter? How can you improve your practice of each of these guidelines?